An
ALL THE YEAR
GARDEN

AN
ALL THE YEAR
GARDEN

MARGERY FISH

CAPITAL
BOOKS, INC.
Sterling, Virginia

CAPITAL BOOKS INC.

First published 1958
By David and Charles (publishers) Limited
Reprinted in 1966, 1971, 1972
Reissued in paperback 2001
By B. T. Batsford

Printed and bound by Bell & Bain Ltd., Glasgow

ISBN 1-892123-68-1

Capital Books Inc.
22841 Quicksilver Drive
Sterling, Virginia 20166

Contents

Foreword

'The garden to strive for is one that has no off-moments but is interesting and attractive whatever the time of year.' So says Margery Fish in her introduction to the original edition of this book. In the 21st century this may seem like stating the obvious but in 1958 it was a more surprising notion. The strength of this book is that it proves the point.

Starting as a gardening journalist then gaining a reputation as a lecturer, Margery caught the attention of more gardeners, and made a more lasting impact, with her first book, *We Made a Garden*. Having completed the tribute to her late husband, in this, her second book, she set out in detail how to achieve her aim of a garden that looks good all the year round.

This is a confident Margery Fish, making her own garden in her own way and writing about it with natural enthusiasm to help gardeners break away from the traditional idea of empty and desolate gardens in winter. In particular she focuses on the plants themselves, highlighting those that can be relied upon to flower in winter, on evergreen foliage plants that fill the garden with long-term interest, and on plants with unusually long seasons of colour.

Recognising that the period from autumn through to the bulbs of spring is the most difficult time for most gardeners planning an all-the-year garden, Margery highlights hellebores and hardy cyclamen, plants which in the 1950s were not considered particularly significant. Through her persuasive prose, based as ever on her own experiences at East Lambrook Manor, she raises them to the first rank. She also stirred interest in heathers as winter flowers, in peat gardening, and her infectious delight in collecting plants, like hellebores and the old hose-in-hose primroses, still delights us.

And all the while, her own appreciation of the way her plants grew and her understanding of how to encourage them to give their best adds fundamental horticultural wisdom to her natural enthusiasm for the plants themselves. This is a book that changed the way we garden.

Graham Rice
2001

Introduction

I think all gardeners have some definite aim as to what they want to achieve in their gardens. Some people are collectors pure and simple, while others want a magnificent floral display from May to September.

Ever since I started gardening, I have felt that the garden to strive for is one that has no off-moments but is interesting and attractive whatever the time of year.

In my first book, *We Made a Garden,* I told how we made our all-the-year-round garden, but there was no space then for details of all the plants for such a garden.

A garden that is to be good always needs careful planting. To get flowers for every day in the year means that no space must be wasted and the plants chosen must have flowering seasons to cover the whole year.

My first thought is for the difficult months from late autumn onwards. Then the hellebores are in bloom, and, if the varieties are selected carefully, they will go on till late May and early June. Violets are not spectacular, but they bloom in the winter and early spring and make welcome groundcover among the shrubs. Spring is the real time for primroses, but they do not stick to rigid rules and many flower in autumn and in mild weather during the winter, when every little flower brings pleasure.

That is why I have devoted a chapter to hardy cyclamen. There are cyclamen for every month in the year, and the ones that bloom in the dark days are just as easy to grow as the summer ones, and often they flower more freely.

Bulbs are not merely a spring-time delight. There are bulbs that can add to the beauty of the garden in every month, and irises, too, can be chosen to furnish flowers for every season.

I always think geraniums are good plants to grow in an all-theyear garden. Most of them have an exceptionally long flowering season, and many have attractive evergreen foliage that colours in autumn and is a blessing throughout the winter.

Flowers that have a long season of blooming have always seemed to me to be worth growing; they can help us through the dull times in the garden, and are usually easy to grow and need little attention.

There was a time when the criterion of a good garden was colour and the vivid colour of massed flowers the main aim. We still want colour, but not necessarily strong colour. I am glad that we have come to appreciate the beauty of foliage in all its colours and textures, because I am convinced that though we love our flowers and wouldn't be without them, it is foliage that gives that settled, finished look that makes a good garden. Silver plants, too, can be as effective as clumps of flowers, but the effect is permanent and gardeners are using silver subjects more and more.

No one could have an all-the-year garden without heathers. There are many that bloom in winter, and though those of us with lime in our soils can grow *Erica carnea* in all its forms and colours, there are many that must have an acid soil. I made my peat garden in the first place so that I could grow all the heathers I wanted, and then I discovered how many other lovely things, many of them winter-flowering, I could grow as well.

Most good gardeners prefer to see their flowers growing rather than picked for the house. But there are ways of having part of your garden indoors without spoiling the outside effect.

I suppose the winter is the best test of a good garden. Spring-time brings its own beauty, and one can be dazzled by the brilliance of summer and autumn; but the winter garden needs careful planning with plants that keep their attractiveness. If I can enjoy a garden in the winter, I am quite certain that it is a good one.

Margery Fish

~ 1 ~

The Winter Garden

I don't think any garden can be considered a success if it does not look pleasant in the winter. There is no difficulty in having an attractive garden at the times of year when there are flowers to help, but though there are a few flowers in the winter, we have to rely mostly on our general lay-out and our evergreen shrubs and herbaceous plants to get a pleasing winter scene.

Of course, some people don't want to go into the garden in the winter. My husband didn't. He had to walk from the garage to the house, but if it was cold he did it hurriedly without a glance to right or left. I know many people who are warm-weather gardeners, and put away their tools at the end of October and wouldn't dream of getting them out again till March.

What a lot they miss! I am glad I am writing this in the middle of January, with the ground white with frost and a pleasant rime on tree and leaf. I have found jobs to do, a few herbaceous things that needed cutting down, a few dead heads on the lilac that should have been cut off long ago, ivy that had started to clamber up the walls and had to be discouraged, and valerian on the outside walls that had not been deprived of its third crop of luxuriant growth. The ground was far too hard for me to weed, but I could stand on the beds without making any impression at all.

Well wrapped against the cold, I found the garden a very exciting place on this winter's day, and I tried to look at it with a stranger's eyes to see what was good and what was bad. I think we all get so used to our own gardens that it is difficult to be critical, and I try from time to time to look at my garden with new eyes.

My aim, then, was to consider which of my garden furnishings stood up best to real wintry weather and gave the garden a comfortable, well-clothed look even in the middle of winter. And as I walked round, there were excitements at every turn.

I read an article the other day in which the writer said he had no use for flowers that bloom in the winter. I agree with him as regards forced flowers. It gives me no pleasure to get daffodils at Christmas or tulips in January. And I think it is real cruelty to leave wreaths of hot-house flowers lying outside in cold frosty weather when holly and evergreens would feel so much better and look so much cosier.

But I love the flowers that bloom in the winter. Each one is a thrill, and I think we get as much pleasure from one tiny bloom on a winter's day as we do from a gardenful of roses in summer.

There were two little aconites peeping out of the grass to greet me as I went into the garden, lovely little things with such big green ruffs under their golden globes. The next flower I saw was my beloved *Cyclamen coum,* twinkling away as if it were midsummer. I met a great many more cyclamen before my day was done, great clumps of white *Cyclamen atkinsii*,* each little flower with its deep crimson blotch. There were pink and crimson *atkinsii*,* too, and under a little cypress a really lovely patch of deep pink *ibericum*.*

On the rock garden, the brilliant blue of *Iris histrioides* dazzled me against its backdrop of pink *Erica carnea.* The lovely blue leaves of *Eucalyptus gunnii* were as beautiful as they are in midsummer, and they fluttered in the cold wintry wind just as they do on a summer's day without any sign of distress. Beyond the wall I met my first hellebore, *Helleborus orientalis,* in a lovely shade of pink, which I think is called 'Apple Blossom'. Nearby was a group of another form, a greenish shade of cream that is so typical of these hellebores.

On the other side of the path in my new planting, the first thing I noticed was a huge rounded bush of *Veronica salicifolia*,* its pale pointed foliage not minding the cold at all and topped by many long spikes of white flowers. Nearby was a small laurustinus, not big enough to flower yet, but nice and green and happy and very pleasant to meet on a winter's day. I am promised a layer of Mr. Bowles's form of *Viburnum tinus,* which I understand is a much twiggier shrub than the usual form, with smaller leaves and innumerable flower clusters with red stalks and scarlet buds. I am told that when it gets going, it is smothered with flower clusters on every twig. I can't wait to get it.

I am trying *Magnolia grandiflora* Exbury form*, in the open in this piece of garden, and I thought how well it looks. There is nothing so handsome as its large shiny leaves, which look as though they were newly unfurled. Near it is an atriplex, to be truthful, rather too near because the atriplex is getting far too big, as atriplexes do. I have cut many of its long stems to use in the house. Why don't more people grow this shrub, with its little leaves of grey satin? It was looking quite happy today, in spite of the intense cold.

I think the most startling feature of this garden is a large planting of the Italian form of *Helleborus foetidus.* While our native form is inclined to sprawl and spread, the one from Italy stands up to face the world. Here I saw a graceful mass of dark cut foliage with wonderful pale green flower trusses held high above. The contrast in the two greens is really most spectacular. The flowers have not yet developed enough to show the purple edgings to their skirts, but they are beautifully finished with bracts and leaves the pale colour of the flowers.

Euphorbia wulfenji is just coming into bloom. All the flower spikes are turned down preparing for this great event, and very soon they will straighten out into great trusses of love-bird green flowers, each with its little black eye. *Cryptomeria* is a lovely winter shrub. I love it in the summer, too, when its soft feathery foliage is a purplish green, but it comes into its own in the winter when it turns russet-red. I think this shrub looks best when planted at the top of a bank, so that it can settle down gracefully over the bank. Mine alas is on level ground, and not nearly so elegant as when it can sweep its graceful branches over a bank.

I have some good groundcover under these shrubs. *Lamium maculatum,* in white and salmon pink, is good all the year round; *Symphytum grandiflorum** is still only dark green, and we have to wait for its hanging cream bells, tipped with orange. Geums look well in winter, and so does the foliage of *Chrysanthemum macrophyllum**, in a delicate shade of green. The Caucasian form* of symphytum makes a handsome clump of large hairy leaves; Jackman's blue rue is untouched by cold, and the new growth of the giant thistle, *Cynara cardunculus,* is about two feet high, two feet of heraldic silver foliage. I have a lot of the green-burred eryngiums in this garden, and their foliage is good in winter, as are the big clumps of *Carex pendula,* a graceful grass, and the great succulent pineapple head of *Kniphofia northiae,* surely like no other kniphofia. White violets are in bloom; *Vinca difformis* is pegging itself down wherever it can find a vacant space with little tufts of shining green foliage; the great red leaves of bergenias hide the little tight pink buds that will soon be open, and *Geranium macrorrhizum* make lovely mounds of red. A small symmetrical clump of *Ballota pseudodictamnus* near by is in splendid contrast with its grey woolly foliage.

There are flowers, too, on 'Harpur Crewe'*, the perennial wallflower that makes a sturdy rounded bush, which is beginning to cover itself with its double golden flowers. There are many blooms on the red pulmonaria, and I see little bits of blue and pink showing above the spotted leaves of *Pulmonaria saccharata* 'Mrs Moon'.

Fat white buds are showing on a japonica (I beg your pardon, chaenomeles) that hugs the wall as I go round to iris corner and see how lovely the red foliage of *Euphorbia sikkimensis* shows up at this time of year. There will soon be flowers on the dark green, evergreen *Euphorbia Robbiae**. I have only just cut off the finished flowers of last year, and now I see the flower-tips are all bent over protecting the buds for this season's flowers.

More violets here, pale blue and coral pink, the sad pink of the Corsican violet and the rich claret of 'Red Queen'. There are the dark crimson-velvet flowers of *Primula* 'David Green' and the brilliant yellow, each with a green eye, of *Polyanthus* 'Barrowby Gem', and there are coloured and pale primroses coming out in every nook and cranny.

More and more hellebores, the blue green of *H. lividus* and the deep maroon of *H. abchasicus** and *H. atrorubens** have been out for a long time, and there are neat clumps smothered in rather small, deep plum flowers. I feel I ought to lay the bark of silver birch on the ground to show up the dark flowers of *H.* 'Black Knight' and 'Ballard's Black', the darkest of them all. The pink of *H.* 'Aurora' shows up well against its fresh green foliage, and near by the darker *H. atrorubens**. *H.* 'Peach Blossom' is a delicious shade of pink, and I always turn up the flowers as I pass by to admire. I think these hellebores, and such plants as Solomon's Seal, should be grown well above the ground. They hang their heads down, and it is difficult to see them without going on one's knees.

Now the Christmas roses do stand up stiffly on stout stems and don't hang their heads so modestly. There has been a great deal of correspondence lately about Christmas roses. To most people there is just *Helleborus niger,* but it is like all other plants—when you get really interested in them you discover what a number there are of each variety. The latest addition to the family is a fabulous giant called 'Potter's Wheel'. It is bigger and better in every way than the ordinary forms of *H. niger* but I haven't had mine long enough to know whether it is going to be the Christmas rose of my dreams, with big flowers on tall stems, which will bloom for me in November. I first saw it in a garden in Porlock, and it certainly dwarfed every other Christmas rose I've ever seen, with enormous flowers of unflushed white. I don't believe it was the result of deliberate hybridizing. The story that came to me was that it had been discovered in a humble garden in the Potteries, hence the name.

I used to have a tiny form of *H. niger,* with flowers much smaller than the average on short stems. With my usual habit of not being able to leave well alone I felt it might do better in another place and I moved it from the niche where it was growing quite happily because I thought it might do better somewhere else. It didn't agree and dwindled away in disgust.

It has always been my ambition to have Christmas roses at Christmas time. Other people do and although I have bought a good many different forms, I haven't yet had early flowers. It makes me envious when I go into the homes of people I know aren't particularly interested in gardening and see bowls of Christmas roses long before Christmas. I can remember seeing them with their own leaves on a farmhouse mantelpiece, in a twinkling copper bowl, above a log fire. In another farmhouse a crystal bowl had been filled with ferny moss and the most perfect flowers I've ever seen looked lovely against that background of moss and leaf.

And while we are talking about hellebores I cannot leave out my favourite of them all, *H. corsicus**. It is not yet out (in the middle of January), but the buds are there and I look forward to the lovely apple-green flowers which I shall have till June. *H. viridis* isn't out either; in fact, the leaves are only just coming through the ground. This is our native hellebore, and it grows wild in some places. The flowers are the darkest green of all, about the same colour as the leaves, but it is not a very generous flowerer with me and does not increase very fast.

A little plant I used to enjoy in the winter was *Lithospermum rosmarinifolium**. I was warned that I should not keep it through the winter, and after a year the prediction came true and I lost it. I haven't given up hope of growing it, however, and wonder if it would come through in the sunny front garden, with its southern aspect and the big chimney with its smouldering wood fire.

As well as the *carnea* ericas, which are growing on the rock gardens, I have some of the winter-flowering ones in the peat garden. There is *darleyensis* in rosy-purple and the snow-white 'W. T. Rackliff'*.

I have an interloper opposite the peat garden. I foolishly allowed a nurseryman to sell me winter heliotrope, *Petasites fragrans,* when I started gardening and knew not what I was taking to my heart. I very soon discovered what I had invited into the garden and spent years trying to get it out of the first place, but made a second, worse mistake and planted it in the ditch under the willows. That part of the garden was wild then, but now I grow my primroses and woodland plants there and I fight a continual war. I tug and pull, and cut and drag, but it retreats behind the stones that hold the bank up and pops out in another place, laughing at me. It doesn't often get a chance to flower, and I don't mind because I get all I want from the roadside; but it has a wonderful time burrowing deeper and deeper into the bank and playing hide-and-seek with me. I wish it had better manners because I like those pale mauve flowers very much. They have an old-world air, with speckled centres and a pink tinge round the edge of the flower. I like the large round leaves, which are such a lovely shade of green, and the little round green buds. The scent is delicious, and I am sure if it was a difficult plant we should all grow it. As it is, I know that when I am dead and gone, it will systematically take possession of my garden.

I don't get as many winter irises as I should because I think I tidy them up too much. They really prefer to be left quite alone to produce their sweet-scented flowers from a tangle of brown leaves and yellow tips. To pull out the dead leaves is resented nearly as much as taking off bits of the plant, and though I get a succession of flowers during the winter months, I don't get the hundreds that come from the thickets of my friends. I do not mind, because I think two or three blooms in a pewter mug with their own foliage are more beautiful than a bowlful. The white ones are particularly lovely, especially the white form *I. unguicularis speciosa**. The dark-flowered forms are lovely, too, and I find the smaller flowers of the tiny *I. unguicularis angustifolia** most exciting.

The first two snowdrops to flower with me, about Christmas-time, are the giant Caucasian snowdrop with large flowers on long stems and *elwesii,* with its very wide and glaucous foliage.

Primroses and primulas come out very early in the year. I have *Primula* 'Wanda' tucked under hedges and at the bottom of stone walls, and she is one of the first to flower. The pale *P. altaica grandiflora** is another early one, and a deep orchid one which I think is *crispli. Polyanthus* 'Barrowby Gem', in pale gold with green eye and a delicious scent, is out in January, and 'Bartimaeus', the one-eyed polyanthus, was blooming in December.

There are always odd flowers out in January, flowers that really have no business to be blooming now, the shaggy little double daisies in pink and white, and odd violas and pansies. *Viola* 'Iden Gem' never stops flowering and there is a little cream one that usually braves the winter. I expect *Othonnopsis cheirifolia** to flower about this time. Its blue-grey fleshy foliage is always good, and the small yellow daisies usually start to flower in January.

I always get a delighted surprise when I meet my leucojums blooming their heads off so early in the year. I had to cut back a rather rampant plant of *Artemisia canescens** which was knocking them about. Why don't we grow more leucojums, I wonder. They come earlier than snowdrops and they are so sumptuous. Their leaves are wide and lush shining green, and the flowers are bigger and fuller, rather like crinolined skirts in glistening white, with pointed, green-tipped petals. There are snowflakes that bloom in the summer and snowflakes that bloom in the autumn, but the one that charms us in the middle of winter, *L. vernum,* is the one for me.

A great deal is written these days about the shrubs that bloom in the winter. I think all gardeners must know about *Prunus subhirtella autumnalis*,* which looks as though a snowstorm had decked the tree, and which I like to gaze at with a wintry sun and blue sky. Witch Hazel is always amusing, with its tiny yellow spider flowers, and later there is *Cornus mas,* with more yellow flowers on bare branches. 1 have dwarf veronica which blooms all through the winter. It was given to me as *V.* 'Morning Glory'*. I have never seen it anywhere except that one garden, nor do I know any nursery that grows it. When I say 'Morning Glory'* people think I mean 'Autumn Glory', which I don't. My little shrub is not so dark in leaf or flower as 'Autumn Glory', it is neater and far more generous with its flowers. I can always cut a bunch from it any day during the winter.

I think *Chimonanthus fragrans*,* Wintersweet, should be near the house so that the wonderful scent from its blossoms can come stealing in when windows are open. People are always belittling the flowers of this shrub, and call them 'dowdy', insignificant or uninteresting. I don't agree. I love to see those waxy blossoms shining in the sunshine, each with an inward glow from the encircling embrace of crimson petals. I put my tree in the corner of the house between south and west walls, but it was a mistake. The position is all right, but there are windows on each wall, and chimonanthus, when she gets going, becomes a very fine girl. To stop her obscuring the windows we have to chop very vigorously, and now I get most of the flowers just below my bedroom windows. Those windows are small and heavily barred with iron, which makes it very difficult for me to cut the little sprigs of scented loveliness I like to put in my mixed bowl.

Another mistake was to plant *Garrya elliptica* bang in front of the sitting-room window. Again it gets big, and has to be cut ruthlessly if all daylight is not to be obscured. And the pruning must be done very early in the year or there will be no lovely green catkins for the winter. I have put another one in with its back to the hedge, because I know the day will come when the old fellow will have to go.

I am not worried about *Daphne laureola,* who lives near by. She may get buxom, but it will be in a dumpy way. Again, I hear people say rude things about her, but I love that dark shining foliage and the tiny green flowers that come in winter and smell so sweet. I agree she is not so showy as her lovely purple-flowered sister and the even lovelier white form, but I think we need shrubs which keep their leaves in winter. That is why I like *Veronica cupressoides*,* which is just as lovely with its blue-grey haze in winter as summer, and has the same aromatic fragrance.

The mahonias are great winter stand-bys. I believe the aristocratic *Mahonia lomariifolium** is not quite as hardy as the others, but I have it growing in a sheltered corner and find it quite hardy. I know it is heresy, but I prefer *M. bealei*,* with its deliciously scented flowers, in greeny yellow. To me the flowers of *M. lomariifolium** are too yellow, too stiff, and have no scent. When we came here there was a mass of *M. aquifolium* growing in the wall at the corner of the front garden. It is a good thing I like to see its shiny dark leaves sprouting out of a high, dreary wall, because it is quite certain I could never get rid of it without pulling the wall down. Later on there will be cheerful yellow flowers, not scented of course, but quite useful for cutting when there isn't much else.

The sarcococcas are not showy plants, but they are neat and green and their tiny cream flowers very pleasant in the winter. On the lower branches there are usually still the fruits, either black or dark red, to add a little more colour. The shrubby polygalas flower with me in the winter, and I am particularly fond of the little cream-and yellow *P. chamaebuxus,* which is so small and cheerful and willing. I don't have the same success with the purple-flowered form, and am *now* trying them in peat, which I think may be the answer.

I used to grow the winter-flowering honeysuckle, but decided that it really did not pay for its keep. I had it on one of my precious south walls, and though I loved its nice green leaves, there were not enough white flowers to go with them; and although I loved the scent of the few I had, I felt I could use that wall to better advantage.

But the common old winter jasmine is allowed to sprawl about on odd walls in different parts of the garden. I don't give up a south wall, of course, she would not expect that, but on any other she does her stuff nobly and flings down her long arms to take root in the ground with the persistence of the bramble.

*Coronilla glauca** comes and goes with me. I sometimes have a fine plant on the south wall near the gate, and enjoy the yellow pea flowers in the winter. Then we have a very bad frost and it is too much for her. I have to beg cuttings from a friend and start all over again, and I think the gamble is worthwhile, because in a good year the effect of gold against blue foliage is really lovely.

I get colour in the garden in other ways. The gold and green of *Elaeagnus pungens aurea-variegata** is as good as a ray of sunshine, and trails of white, pink and green ivy pegged along the ground are gay and clean. And so is *Euonymus* 'Silver Queen'*, which I use as ground cover, too, and the variegated bugle, which has a pink tint in the winter. Bergenias, tellima and some of the heucheras turn crimson in the cold, and as contrast there is the grey-green, ferny foliage of *Anthemis cupaniana*,* the dark green of hymenanthera and *Osmanthus delavayi,* and the various colours of the little conifers I have in the garden.

Phormium in green or red brings a new note, and there is grey and green in the different rosemaries. The silver leaves of globe artichokes are lovely for many a long day.

I planted a *Cotoneaster lactea** to cover the uninspiring walls of a new pantry and other offices, and I could not have found anything to do the job better. This is one of the evergreen cotoneasters, and grows well and gracefully. It is covered with hanging tresses of red berries from autumn onwards, not the bright berries of *C. horizontalis* or the pyracanthas, but berries of soft crimson with a matt finish. I get annoyed sometimes when I find seedlings of this cotoneaster in places where I don't want them and from which I have difficulty in removing them, but the sight of that back-drop of green and crimson hiding the plainness of domesticity soon makes me forgive.

Another climber that I enjoy in the winter is *Clematis calycina**. It is not very showy, in fact, one has to hunt for the small greenish-yellow flowers among the bronze tangle of ferny leaves; but I like this visitor from Minorca, and grow it over the wall near the gate.

We all know and love *Viburnum fragrans*,* either as a tall shrub trained against a wall or a neat little bush among the flowers. The pink-flowered *V. bodnantense* is said to be a more vigorous shrub, with more and bigger flowers. *V. burkwoodii* begins flowering with me in February, and *V. utile,* which I have against the malt-house wall, is rather more open in its growth, but it, too, keeps its dark glossy leaves all through the winter, to make a lovely pattern against a light wall.

I think skimmias are among the nicest shrubs to have in the garden for winter enjoyment if you can arrange their domestic life satisfactorily. I thought I had achieved a very happy solution by planting two couples close together, so that if one member of the community passed on there would still be adequate companionship for the survivors. But for some reason they did not like the position I gave them, and three of them died and I was left not knowing if I had a widow or a widower on my hands.

Another couple that were given to me, I planted on each side of the shallow steps leading to the wide terrace. Madame is very buxom and produces wonderful berries, which the birds don't appear to enjoy, but Monsieur gets more pale and anxious every year and is plainly wasting away. I am debating a little match-making with the lonely spouseless plant round the corner, and may in that way discover the sex of the triply bereaved.

~ 2 ~
Hellebores

All addicts are liable to become bores unless they are talking to people with the same form of fanaticism. Hellebores are very exciting to those who like them, and I notice they keep cropping up in conversation and writing, which makes me think that more and more people are realizing what excellent plants they are. For an all-the-year-round garden there is nothing to beat them, because they produce flowers from November to June, the months when there aren't so many flowers in bloom.

Everybody knows the Christmas rose, and I am always surprised how well many people grow them; people who are not particularly garden-minded, who don't have particularly interesting things in their gardens, and who see gardening in the right perspective, not regarding it as all-important, as some of us do.

I try terribly hard with my Christmas roses, *Helleborus niger* to give it its proper name, but mine don't begin to compare with those of many people I know. I do all the things that appeal to them, planting them in deep rich soil, where they won't be disturbed, mulching them in summer, and watering them when it is dry. And when the first buds appear I cover them up with wooden boxes that have windolite instead of wood at the top, so as to get pure, unsullied flowers on long stems. My flowers are never as big or as perfect or as early as some that are left to bring themselves up, and I am faced again with the fact that those who fuss too much don't always get the best results. I am sure my successful friends, many of them humble folk with one plant in their gardens to the hundreds in mine, don't worry about the different species that I buy hoping to get the super-early blooms I crave. *H. niger altifolius** is one I bought, which is very similar to *H. macranthus**. It should start flowering in November and has pink shading on the outside of its petals, and the flowers are borne on very long stems. There used to be a good one called the St Brigid Christmas rose, but I don't often hear of it now.

Though I don't do well with *H. niger,* I have no complaints about *H. orientalis,* called Lenten roses because they flower in the spring. They also flower in the autumn with me, and I can usually find a few blooms in late November. The late ones go on till April and May, and their evergreen foliage makes them more than ever welcome in the garden. I don't know how other people fare, but they do extremely well for me and don't seem to mind whatever I do to them. I am sure if I dug up my *H. niger* in the middle of its flowering, left it lying about on my work bench until it was flabby and insensitive enough for me to wriggle the clump apart into half a dozen crowns, even sever them with a knife where necessary, they would so resent it that they would never speak to me again. Yet the forgiving Lenten roses bear no malice. After their ordeal on the operating table, they let themselves be replanted and go on blooming where they left off. Even tiny shoots that sometimes get broken in the process soon grow into nice little plants in boxes of sandy compost.

Most of the Lenten roses I grow have no names; they vary in colour from white and pale green to deepest plum colour. 'Black Knight' is one of the darkest and *orientalis* one of the palest, and incidentally one of the first to flower. 'Apple Blossom' and 'Peach Blossom' are what you would expect from such names, and *odorus* is primrose coloured and scented. *H. abchasicus** is maroon, and *guttatus** has a multitude of small crimson dots on a greeny cream ground. It is practically the same as an old one called 'Prince Rupert'; in fact, I think they are probably one and the same. But all the Lenten roses are beautiful though hard to match up. The colours vary according to the length of time the flowers are open, and some of them last a very long time if left growing. I seldom pick them because they do not last long indoors, even if one does slit their stem from the throat downwards, but I allow myself a few heads in a shallow bowl, so that I can enjoy their shadings and stipplings, the beautifully packed stamens in the centre and the surrounding circle of translucent green nectaries, which show themselves under the microscope as perfect open tubes.

My Lenten roses do well in several places in the garden. In the small front garden I have hydrangeas under the north wall and plant the hellebores among them, so that when the hydrangeas finish, the hellebores take over. Near the orchard I have several large beds which are just shady enough for these lovely plants. At one time these beds were paved because they were not big enough to grass over and I wanted something that was easy to look after. A keen gardening friend, whose opinion I value, remarked one day that these beds would be a good place for primulas, so up came the paving, down went the compost and now I grow there *Primula sieboldii,* fat candelabra primulas, and my handsome hellebores. They are in bloom from November till May, beginning with *H. orientalis* and a lovely pink, and ending with a greenish white that doesn't show a bud till March.

The lovely green-flowered *H. foetidus* is the next to flower. I love its handsome dark cut foliage, which is evergreen and a wonderful contrast to the pale green flowers. Though the flowers themselves do not come to their full maturity until early in the year, the plants become interesting about the end of November with the pale green buds nestling among young leaves of the same colour. I think there are two distinct forms of *H. foetidus*. The one that is sometimes found growing wild in English woods is rather sprawling in habit and looks best among stones or in a corner. The Italian form is more erect and stands about one and half feet to two feet, with the sprays of flowers rising above. The flowers of *H. foetidus* are rather small and handsome, a little paler than *H. corsicus** and much paler than *H. viridis*. After they have been out for a short time, a dark purple margin appears at the edge of the petals, giving the effect of little dark petticoats below the pale green flowers. I have never detected an unpleasant smell from this plant; it is certainly not as 'stinking' as other families that bear the same degrading Latin name, but the seeds, at any rate, have poisonous properties. A friend of mine who has large patches of it found her fingers and thumb covered in big blisters after she had collected a quantity of seed.

I think if I could grow only one hellebore, I should choose *H. corsicus**. The only reason why I should ever want to go to Corsica would be to see these majestic hellebores in their natural setting. I don't know how big they are, but I doubt if any of them are as fine as one I have growing in the north-east corner of my front garden.

It is planted next to a *Hydrangea macrophylla mariesii**, and at the moment I am able to play 'Box and Cox' with them quite happily, but I can't think what will happen when they get even bigger. When the hydrangea is in bloom I tie *H. corsicus** back to the wall with very heavy tarred string, and when *H. mariesii** has nothing to show but bare bones I loosen the bonds round *corsicus** so that she can stretch herself, and I can enjoy the full beauty of her heraldic foliage and watch the trusses of flower-buds developing. *Corsicus** has the finest flowers of the green-flowered tribe, large open blooms in pale apple green. I can never bring myself to pick a whole truss of flowers because I enjoy the sight of them from my desk from December to June, but I allow myself the odd flower now and again to put in a low bowl and enjoy indoors. The seed of *H. corsicus** germinates well if it is sown the moment it is ripe. I watch my seed-pods with an eagle eye, and even spread sheets of paper under the plant when they are nearly ready to spill their shiny black seeds, so that none shall escape me.

There is one thing I have discovered about *H. corsicus**, and that is not to pamper her with rich living. Too much manure or compost has a bad effect, and if indulged in too much will shorten her life. I don't imagine there are many luxuries on the stony island of Corsica, and over-indulgence in the good things of life is fatal.

I can't write with so much assurance about *H. lividus*. I believe this species is the only hellebore that may not be quite hardy. I have had mine only for a few years, and there has not been a really hard winter since she came to live with me.

I have given her a sheltered site, with plenty of protection by hedges, and she seems to be getting along all right. She flowers, but not very prolifically; and after flowering, her flower stalks and then her leaves began to wither away. I almost sat up at nights holding her hand, but there was really nothing I could do. Then I noticed new growth beginning to show, and my hopes went up, only to be dashed a day or two later when I discovered that slugs were eating off the new leaves as soon as they appeared. I had a real slug warfare, with everything in the cupboard in the way of slug poisons, and a barricade of ashes round the precious creature to deter snails. By degrees I pulled her round, and she is still with me, though not as blooming as I would like. I give this hellebore plenty of peat and sand; I don't think it detests lime as much as some plants, but it doesn't care for it as much as the other hellebores, and prefers a fairly light soil, hence the sand. *H. lividus* is not as tall as the other hellebores, and there is a blue haze about her. The foliage is blue-green, and so are the flowers, in a more delicate tone. A friend gave me my plant, and I think she was very brave to divide such a treasure. Since she gave me my piece, she has taken courage in both hands and divided her large clump into small pieces without any ill-effects. The textbooks recommend July as the best month for dividing hellebores, but I have never felt they minded being divided at other times of the year, and I often pull my Lenten roses to pieces just before they begin to flower. I don't know if other growers are more successful in getting seed from *H. lividus.* When my flower stems drooped and withered, I realized my hopes of raising a family of little *lividi* had gone too, so I am glad to think division is not out of the question.

Our second native hellebore, *H. viridis,* is the last of all to come into flower. When the other members of the family are blooming their heads off, the neatly furled leaves of *H. viridis* are just beginning to push through the ground. This hellebore disappears completely during the summer, and I never rest easy until I see the new leaves coming through some time after Christmas. They are very bright and shining, and the flowers are as green as the leaves, rather small and open. Some knowledgeable gardening friends took me with great pride to show me their green anemone, and I hated to have to tell them that their *rara avis* was not an anemone but a hellebore. Though this hellebore does grow wild in various parts of the country, I think one would have to penetrate deeply into a wood or copse to find any quantity. A friend of mine who lives in Shropshire has some very fine clumps growing in a chicken-run, and generously dug me up a lump. The chickens were poking and scratching among the roots, which were clinging tenaciously to the hard, trodden earth; but they were much more interested in worms and mercifully left the hellebores quite alone.

Though the flowers of *H. viridis* are small and do not show up well, they are as exquisitely formed as all the hellebore flowers. The petals are pointed and symmetrical, and neatly arranged nectaries of the same deep green are clustered round the tightly packed stamens.

H. viridis starts flowering about March, and goes on till May and June, so that if one collects cleverly, there can be hellebores blooming in the garden from November to midsummer, and only four months without them.

~ 3 ~

Violets

I don't know if my part of the world is better for violets than any other; one often hears about Devon violets and Dorset violets, but Somerset can hold her own with either of them. Certainly they grow in our woods and banks and in most of the gardens. Long before Christmas, perhaps even in October, the villagers have little bunches of purple violets in their buttonholes, violets that they have picked from their cottage gardens. The violets are not planted there, they just arrive, but they don't get in anyone's way; in fact, I think they are a very welcome form of ground cover, and their sweetness is there for all who'll take it.

I believe there are banks and hedges where white violets grow in our countryside, but I haven't found them. The trouble of giving your heart to a garden is that there is always so much to do in it that there is never time to roam the countryside. When we first came to live in Somerset I had several treats I allowed myself each year. The first was to go looking for marsh marigolds. There are several low-lying fields where they grow, but my favourite haunt is a small waterlogged piece of land near the River Parrott. It is at the end of a little lane, and there is nothing else there but a mill and wild birds. I always felt I was near the sea when I put on my gumboots and squelched among the reeds. A hot sun and a blue sky and the swirling gulls above me were really exciting enough without the armful of marigolds, like lacquered gold, with their fat round buds and succulent leaves.

Another treat was to go picking early orchids, 'single gulls' as the villagers call them. They come into bloom just as the primroses are finishing. The children love to pick them, and the signal for my excursion was the sight of a bunch of orchids crammed in a paste jar sitting in a cottage window. The field was reached through somebody's lane which led to somebody else's orchard, and then a perilous trip down a lane under arching trees, picking one's way over flat stones that rock in the oozing clay. A sharp knife is best to cut the flowers so that the plant will bloom again next year, and a little basket holds the fragrant blooms that range from deep orchid to pale pink. Every year I feared my trip might be the last, because I might reach the field and find it had been ploughed up. Nowadays I seldom seem to manage to pick any orchids; I don't know whether it is that I have acquired so many more plants in the garden that I need all my time for tending them, or it may be that my standards are higher and I have always more work than time.

But to return to our violets: I grow a good many varieties and these seed themselves all over the garden. I wait for them to flower, and then firmly wrest them from their chosen site and replant them with their fellows. I never find a wild purple violet in my garden although I grow the single white, but our native dog violet fancies itself as a garden plant. I have no place quite suitable for these little strangers, so disarming but also without scent, so often I am weak and leave them where they sow themselves. Not so the purple-leaved *V. labradorica**, which I admit as a recognized member of my garden society, and which has larger, deeper blue flowers and lovely purple leaves on long sprays. A good clump of this violet is extremely handsome, and delightful used with light green plants or shrubs.

I can't remember when I first got 'Governor Herrick' and the 'Princess of Wales'*, both deep purple, one scented and one not. For as long as I can remember I have had them clambering up between the stones that hold up the banks of my ditch. They flower from January onwards, and I can never resist picking a little posy when I see them. But I know I don't get as many blooms as I should if I planted them in a frame, and the flowers would be bigger. But I haven't enough frames for everything I would like to shelter, and the violets just have to do the best they can for me out of doors.

I'd like even better to give my double violets the comfort of a frame. It would be wonderful to have bowls full of fragrant double blooms, but I don't think frames add to the beauty of the garden and I have no place where I can hide them away. A friendly antique dealer gave me my first double—the very old 'Duchesse de Parme', with small yellow-green leaves and pale lavender flowers. Then I met 'Marie Louise'* and realized I must have her, too. The flowers are larger and are deeper in colour, and the foliage is finer, too. The double white, 'Comte de Brazza', seems to like my garden, and now I am trying to please another double, a pinky-mauve this time, called 'Mrs John J. Astor'.

Semi-double violets fascinate me, particularly the 'Duchess of Sutherland'. She is a real thoroughbred, long and rangy in growth, with large dark green leaves. The flowers are large and blue, as one would expect from the daughter of the 'Princess of Wales'*. In the centre of each flower is a little ruffle of pink petals. The other semi-doubles are lovely but not quite so exciting as Madame the Duchess. 'Princess Mary' is blue, with a blue rosette centre, and 'Mrs David Lloyd George' is blue, too, with a gold centre.

The 'Czar' is a good violet-coloured violet, not as fine as 'Bournemouth Gem' and 'Governor Herrick', but bigger than the purple form of *Viola odorata*. The white form is the biggest single scented white violet I know; it has large leaves and is a particularly good doer.

The various cultivated forms of *Viola odorata* fascinate me more than any other kinds. Whether they are the result of hybridizing or are chance seedlings, I do not know, but, judging by the number of delightful variations I get in my seedlings, I incline to the latter theory. *V. odorata alba** is a bigger edition of our native white violet. Constant division, generous feeding, and watering in dry weather produce bigger blooms on longer stalks. It seeds itself with me most generously, and as I try to keep one colour to one part of the garden, I can usually be certain what colours I have. I always wait with excitement for the seedlings to flower because I never know what lovely sports I shall get. If they are obvious offspring of one of my regular lines, they are lifted and put back with mother, and the new ones get a place all to themselves, with plenty of compost so that they will increase for me.

The pink *Viola odorata* 'Coeur d'Alsace' is the most beautiful, I think. It is such a deep warm pink, with none of your wishy-washy pale mauve tints in it. It flowers very early, often in October and right through to the spring, and I find it so delightful to find these heavenly scented, heavenly coloured little flowers blooming away in the depths of winter that I often dig up the whole root and enjoy the fragrance and colour indoors. Such treatment doesn't deter them in the least, and they are none the worse when they go back into the garden.

I had my first scrap of the cream-coloured *Viola sulphurea** about ten years ago, and it is my fault that it has remained just the one clump. Now that I am taking trouble with it, dividing it regularly and giving it nice things to eat, it is increasing industriously and seeds itself mildly. The colour is a deep rich cream with a tiny orange eye. There is a deeper form, *V. sulphurea* 'Irish Elegance', which is almost pale apricot.

I have never met the red-purple *V.* 'Admiral Avellan'* in any other garden, and I don't know why. It is one of the most prolific bloomers in this tribe, the stems are long, the scent is strong, and the foliage rather fresher in colour than some of the others. It, too, often begins blooming before Christmas, and it is very seldom that I cannot pick a small bunch from it any time from November onwards.

The violet that is called 'Red Queen' isn't red at all, at least not my idea of red. Wine describes it better, but you couldn't have a Wine Queen! The nearest I can get to a colour description is to compare it with the little 'red' periwinkle, *Vinca minor rubra*, which is the same shade of purplish claret. But even if it is not properly named, I like 'Red Queen' very much. The Corsican violet is not unlike it, but without the sparkle. This again, is difficult to describe, and the nearest I can get to the colour is what I'd call a sad pink.

There are several blue violets. I have a seedling that is a soft China blue; Norah Church is a deeper blue, 'John Raddenbury' is a good blue, and there is another almost sky blue that is said to have come from the Mount of Olives. The violet known as 'French Grey' is really a very pale washed-out blue, or perhaps you'd rather I called it blueish white. The flowers are particularly fine and there are fine big leaves to go with it.

The Christmas violet is one of the smallest. I don't know why it is called Christmas, because it doesn't usually bloom as early as that, and I think the other name 'Skim Milk' suits it better. There is a thin milky look about this fragile flower, smaller than *odorata alba** and with none of the purple shadings of that flower. I like the slight greenish tinge in its hooded petals, and the very pale green of the calyx, and the modest way the little plant creeps about, covering the soil and giving its tender little flowers.

Devon violets are real violets, very sweetly scented, rather small, and a real violet colour. I am assured they are the same as Russian violets, but can never understand how this can be, unless the name Russian has crept in by the back door. I wanted mine to get busy and increase quickly, so I planted them with plenty of peat and a dash of sand, and they have responded in a remarkable way. I think all violets enjoy a little attention: manure, compost, or peat, and certainly they don't like to get dried out in summer.

There are two really yellow violets that I know, unscented alas, but very charming. The tiny alpine *V. biflora* comes from Austria and Switzerland, and is usually found growing many thousand feet up. It doesn't seem to mind living in the lowlands, and isn't at all choosy about position and soil, although it mustn't be too dry. It disappears completely in the winter, and I fear sometimes gets weeded up. The other one disappears, too, but bobs up smilingly every year. It is *V. pensylvanica**, a little larger than *biflora* with golden, very shining leaves.

Viola seprentrionalis comes from Arkansas in America. It is quite attractive in a large white way, and has delicate etchings of blue in the centre of the flowers. I like my violets to be scented, and this one has no scent at all; nor is it evergreen, as are most of the tribe. All that can be seen in the winter are nobbly crowns, just above the surface of the ground.

~ 4 ~
Bulbs

I think we connect bulbs with the spring because there are more then than in any other time of year, but there are, in fact, bulbs we can use in the garden in every month of the year.

Everyone has their own ideas of what kinds of daffodils, tulip, and gladioli they want to grow in their gardens. There are so many lovely ones, and even lovelier ones are brought out every year so I really don't know where we are ever to stop.

Luckily I am easily pleased, and 'Beersheba' pleases me as well as any daffodil I know. It is not new and there are bigger and better white ones now, but I remain faithful to 'Beersheba', my first love among the whites. I like white daffodils because I think if one wants to include a few groups in the flower-beds, white ones are the best to choose because they are happy with anything. Also I love white daffodils against the old oak panelling of the dining-room, so 'Beersheba' is the girl for me, although I admit the dainty little 'W. P. Milner' runs her a close second. Yellow daffodils, I think, must be planted in grass if they are not to look too rich; but I make an exception in the case of one very small and very early little golden daffodil. I don't know it's name, it is bigger than the rock one we call *nanus,* and has more body and form than the little wild daffodils. It came years ago from my mother's garden, and we all cherish it and call it 'Mother's little daffodil'.

As daffodils of all kinds look their loveliest growing in grass, we have to think of something else to give a little early colour in the flowerbeds, and so we usually choose tulips. I like the soft pink of 'Clara Butt', and a pale pale yellow, with a hint of green. One I admire particularly is 'Niphetos', which is more cream than yellow, with a tinge of green. I think white tulips are arrestingly beautiful in a cool, dignified way, and stand up well in the riot of aubrieta and polyanthus of early spring. 'Ivory Gem' is pure and dignified, and reminds me of warm marble. To get the most from them, I think tulips should be planted in clumps, with the bulbs rather close together, not stretched out in a long row, as one so often sees them. In a clump the colour is concentrated, and that is what we are aiming at.

I plant my tulips rather deeply, and leave them in the ground to save labour. I find that they are not idle, but increase very plcasantly. The size of the grown-up bulbs does not decrease, as the Jonah's prophesy, but one occasionally gets a few youngsters in the clump which turn it into a pleasant family party. Though I leave my tulips in the ground all the year round, I know I take a risk in so doing, because it is so easy and so distressing to spear them with one's fork when they are dormant. If possible, it is safest to plant all bulbs by themselves with good groundcover to hide the naked earth. But there are some, like the tulips, that cannot be left out of the borders if one wants the touches of gaiety they bring.

Crocuses, I think, should always be planted in grass, rough grass that doesn't get cut with a mowing machine, if possible. If planted in lawns, it is politic to group them round a tree so that only a small circle of grass need be left uncut till the crocus foliage dies down. Husbands, who usually either cut the grass or supervise its cutting, get very peevish about the lovely things we plant in the lawn. My husband would not permit any bulbs in the grass, and I knew he would have carried out his threat to cut them off with the first mowing had I dared to disobey. It is only since his death that I have daffodils and crocuses, snowdrops, grape hyacinths, and erythroniums, growing in the sacred lawns.

*Crocus tomasinianus** is the earliest to flower. It comes in lovely shades of blue, mauve, and violet, and responds enthusiastically to the first gleams of wintry sunshine by opening its petals to that welcome warmth. Many lovely ones come later, mauve and violet, yellow and orange. I am addicted to a lovely white person called 'Snowdrift'. She is bolder than most of them, and makes a dazzling show in dew-drenched grass.

All the crocuses seed themselves generously, which is another reason why they are better naturalized. You may think they are safely tucked away in a corner of the rock garden, but when you find seedlings coming up in the middle of your choicest plants, you don't love them quite so much.

Scillas and aconites can be poked into all kinds of odd places. They look lovely under shrubs, of course, and I like them in small pockets at the bottom of walls and at the side of stone paths, where they can be left undisturbed to multiply. One of the most beautiful scillas is *tubergeniana**, rather a chubby little soul in the most beautiful Wedgwood blue. Chionodoxas can be used in the same way, varying the theme with the soft pink of *C. luciliae* 'Pink Giant'* or *C. luciliae alba**, through various shades of blue to the deep *C. sardensis*. Tritelias, with their pale starlike faces, have a sweet scent if you trouble to kneel to them, and they flower very early in the year.

Of the muscari family, my favourite is the neat little plant called *Hyacinthus azureus** by botanists although we know it as a muscari. It is such a beautiful sky blue, and it knows how to control its foliage. The white form, *H. praecox album**, is just as entrancing—and tidy, but I must admit that the tangled leaves of the taller species rouse considerable venom in me for a long time before the exquisite little blue heads thrust their way through the untidy mass. Then I think it was worth suffering the eyesore, but the amnesty is short-lived, for one has to live with the dying foliage for a long time after the flowers have gone. Yes, I think the tall muscari should be used as underplanting in a shrub garden where its uncombed locks will merge with the rather shaggy background. Some people contend that if planted in a lawn or bank where the grass is kept cut, the foliage does not grow so prodigiously, and is, in fact, no worse than that of crocuses after flowering. The feather hyacinth, *Muscari comosum monstrosum**, is quite a respectable citizen so far as its foliage is concerned, and its great violet plumes are welcome in any part of the garden.

Two charming South African bulbs for rock work or other informal places are rhodohypoxis and *Lapeyrousia cruenta**. The first has small flowers of vivid cerise, pink and white. It comes up regularly each year for me, but doesn't increase as I should like it to. They like a well-drained position, but don't want to get too dry in the summer, and I am now trying them in the peat garden, which is cool and moist. A friend told me that she had been able to divide her rhodohypoxis after they had sojourned in peat for a season or two. Lapeyrousia, with its orange flowers, is easier, and if it likes you, will increase quite rapidly. Planted in a bed, it soon wanders on to a nearby path. I use it in crevices in paving, being careful not to plant it where traffic is heavy, and I am now trying to establish colonies in narrow beds between path and low wall and in the rock garden.

There are several summer-flowering bulbs sometimes planted in perennial borders, which would really look better in a less formal seting. The tall white *Galtonia candicans* looks lovely with shrubs as a background for its green-tipped flowers. I have seen it interplanted with polyanthus roses, and it was not a success. If there is no shrub garden, a clump here and there among tall-growing perennials is very pleasant. I am very fond of the delicate green *Galtonia princeps,* and give it a quiet shady corner where it can be undisturbed but still get quite a lot of attention. It doesn't grow quite so tall for me as its showy white sister, and the fragile greenness of its hanging bells is delightful.

The camassias can be used in the same way. I admit the dark blue variety to my borders because it does stay where it is planted, but the light blue one is a prolific creature, increases with great rapidity and comes up all over the garden. A friend of mine planted it in colonies in a really wild part of her garden, where long grass and giant oaks bordered a quiet stream, and the effect was really exceptionally lovely. The Bermudian snowdrop is another subject for the shrub or woodland garden. There, one would enjoy the wealth of green, the nice shiny leaves, and the long and graceful stems, with pretty but ineffectual little white flowers at the ends of them. There is a better one called 'Gravetye Giant', in which the flowers are more in proportion to the rest of the plant. I have always grown the Bermudian snowdrop and I wouldn't think of my garden without it, but for years I have felt I had planted it in too conspicuous a place. I still think it should be more in the background, but I feel differently about it since I was unexpectly left to cope with the church flowers very early one year. A background of faded crimson, dreadful little brass vases with narrow necks, and practically nothing out in the garden made me feel very hopeless about it. It was against my principles to buy flowers, and I struggled with *Garrya elliptica,* which wasn't bad, *Prunus autumnalis*,* which I thought would be so good and didn't show up at all but which I should have continued to use had I not noticed tiny white buds on those long and graceful snowdrop stems. By that time there were a few daffodil buds big enough to pick, and the arching curves of the snowdrops, *Leucojum aestiveum,* redeemed their stiffness and transformed the uncompromising vases.

Another summer bulb which I like to have in the garden but not in the border is *Scilla peruviana,* sometimes called the Cuban lily. Strange to say, it comes from the Mediterranean, so I don't know where it got its names. Its deep blue flowers come in great umbels on ten-inch stems above large glossy leaves, which never die down.

Alliums can be had in all colours and heights by anyone who can stand the smell of onions from the great *giganteum,* with its huge spherical heads of purple, to the tiny rock-garden species. *A. caeruleum* is one of the best, compact and deep cornflower blue, and I wouldn't be without the good-tempered *A. mollis*,* with its yellow mop-heads. It doesn't seed itself so persistently as some others of the tribe. The rare ones, of course, hardly ever oblige with a seedling.

A plant I am fond of is *Tulbaghia violacea,* with its onion scent. It gives a succession of pale mauve flowers on ten-inch stalks until the frosts come, and the foliage is a pleasant glaucous foil for the flowers. I grow mine against a south wall on the top stratum of a rock garden, where it multiplies with great zest.

I do not grow the ordinary gladioli, although I often wish I had the welcome colour they give in late summer. To me their proper place is in the kitchen garden, as they are needed most for picking, although I have seen them most effectively grown in self-coloured clumps among shrubs. To me they are rather unwieldy and difficult to place among ordinary flowers, but among the shrubs one sees only their heads and the effect is charming.

The two gladioli I do grow are the wild purple, *G. byzantinus*,* and a beautiful South African, *G. tristis grandis*.* I don't remember how I first acquired my purple friend; I know I shall never lose it, as it seeds itself everywhere. When it first comes out it is most beautiful, with the loveliest sheen on those fine-textured magenta-ish petals, and elegant length and slimness. It doesn't last long and I spend my days pulling off the spent petals. I have some in the front garden posed in front of *Ceanothus veitchianus**, and as they both come out at the same time, the effect is lovely. I remember seeing a single bloom in a garden in Scotland, and thinking that if it were rare or difficult we should cherish it. Much as I like it, I think its real home should be the woodland garden, where it could seed to its heart's content and would be praised for its endeavours and never blamed.

Gladiolus tristis grandis is another story. She has never seeded herself for me, and many years she has not even flowered. I knew a garden where they grew in dozens round the door of a summer-house, and the scent of those creamy white flowers on a summer evening was intoxicating. But one bad winter came and they were all gone, so they do need care and shelter. The foliage is more like that of a rush than a gladiolus, and it seems to be evergreen. It is safest to plant them behind something taller, as there is no body in these long rushes and they sometimes fall over and the ends get damaged—disastrous when a bud is forming, as thin and unlike a gladiolus as the rush itself. I have them planted in various parts of the garden for many years and get flowers on many of them. So far they have not multiplied for me, but I am grateful that they are still in the garden.

The ordinary orange montbretia is suitable only for a wild garden or the beds bordering a long dull drive, where great patches of flame are exciting in the autumn. 'Antholyza', on the other hand, with its wide leaves and noble branching flower-heads is a magnificent creature when given ample room in a big border. I was recently given a couple of corms of *M.* 'Solfaterre'*, a lovely bronze-leaved montbretia, with pale apricot flowers, wider and bigger than the average. For years I have grown *M. rosea**, so delicate in colour and growth, but entrancingly lovely. It is not a plant to put anywhere and forget. I think it needs a good sunny position, and a little support for those thin and wiry stems. It is South African, but it does not need lifting each autumn as some of the new and dazzling beauties do, but it needs dividing regularly, as do all montbretia.

There are many lovely bulbs for autumn. Most people know colchicum, meadow saffron, and very often they are called 'autumn crocuses', although there are about a dozen and half real crocuses that flower in the autumn. I often wish I had a wild garden, if only so that I could grow all the different forms of colchicum, mauve and white, purple, and single and double. I have mine on the lowest strata of the rock garden, but it is not a perfect place. It is all right when those lovely naked blooms rise like marble statues from the autumn earth, but in the spring one pays for that beauty by great cabbage growth of flabby leaves, which seem to take an inordinate time dying off. I can't plant the bulbs in the grass, as it all gets cut in the spring, and I know no suitable place for my treasures, so I suppose they will continue swamping a large patch of *Convolvulus* *mauritanicus**, which has spread all over the pocket where they grow. The real autumn crocuses, of which there are many lovely colours and kinds, are treated as the spring-flowering ones, and I try to find a home for them where they can be safe for the rest of the year.

Larger than the crocuses, and usually later to flower, are South African Sternbergias, which look very much like crocuses. The glistening globes of yellow come up between strap-like leaves of dark green. They do well in a hot, dry place, with good drainage, and, like the colchicums, they don't mind being lifted just before they are due to flower.

Another good bulb for September and October is Zephyranthes, the flower of the west wind. It is quite hardy and from four to ten inches high. *Z. candida,* the pure white, is the most usual one grown. It has orange stamens and a forest of rushlike foliage. The lemon-coloured form is also an autumn flowerer, while the pink blooms in the summer.

People are now coming to realize the many good points of Kaffir lilies, *Schizostylis*, to give them their proper name, but they have still not become really popular as a cut flower, and I cannot think why. They increase so readily and need only the protection of cloches to ensure speedy opening (that is if they were being grown commercially), and they last in water a very long time. The first to open is *S. coccineus,* a vivid scarlet. There is a bigger form, *S. giganteum*,* which will grow to nearly four feet in a damp, sunny position. 'Professor Barnard' is named after its discoverer, and it is more carmine than scarlet, with rather more open flowers.

The next to flower is 'Mrs Hegarty', which is my favourite and I think the best. The flowers are a lovely shade of deep shell pink; she is not as fleshy as 'Viscountess Byng', and the flowers are rather bigger. 'Viscountess Byng' is the last of all to flower, and if there is an exceptionally early frost she does not always make it. I like to plant her in a sheltered corner so that she can flower in peace. Her flowers are very pale pink, almost like pink satin, and her stems are thick and sturdy.

I am certain that to get good Kaffir lilies they should be divided every year. I like to plant mine out in a light soil, with a little sand added to encourage new roots, and some dried blood to feed them up. Kaffir lilies that are not divided regularly become a solid mat, with miserable short foliage and thin flower heads, quite different from the bouncing beauties that have had proper treatment.

Three other autumn bulbs are crinums, nerines, and belladonna lilies. All like sun and do best under a south wall. For the crinums I'd choose a south wall in the kitchen garden, unless the garden is a very big one that can stand a tropical jungle of rather untidy foliage. Crinums get as big as footballs, and they grow leaves in proportion. The flowers are white, pink, or white shaded with pink, most handsome and delightful, especially when rescued from their overpowering background of vegetation.

Belladonna lilies take a long time to start flowering; in fact, for several years after they are planted you feel you've wasted your time and money. True, every spring will see a little tuft of leaves, which come up neatly packed on top of each other like bus tickets, but in vain you scan the bare soil in the autumn for that red-skinned snout that heralds the lily flower, which may be any shade from pale pink to deep crimson. Once they start flowering, you might think they'd appear regularly year after year, but, alas, this is not so. There will nearly always be a few blooms, but it requires a good, hot summer to encourage a really fine display of bloom. In spite of the loveliness of the flowers, I always think there is something rather inelegant about these naked lilies, which are not really lilies at all, but amaryllis, and I wish they'd arrange to have a few leaves come through the soil with them!

Nerines, on the other hand, though by no means prodigal with leaves, are not born without them entirely. Like the belladonnas, they produce most of their foliage in the spring, and unlike the belladonnas, they do flower very generously, and once they start they have no second thoughts. Nerines have a more lively beauty than the other two. They are deeper in colour, a vivid cerise pink usually, although salmon and shell pinks have been added to the colour range. The petals are narrower and curled, and the flowers more starlike, heavily stamened, and grow in umbels on eighteen-inch stems. There is something rather exotic and hot-housy about them that makes the proud owner wonder, 'Did I really grow that lovely thing?'

A lot has been written about acidantheras during the last few years. Nurserymen extol their virtues, but they don't tell us how difficult they are to flower. They come so late that it is often a race between them and the frost, and I sometimes wonder if we shouldn't do better if we grew them in a greenhouse and thus avoid the yearly anxiety. The buds look so promising, but will they open to lovely white flowers, so deliciously scented and heavily blotched with chocolate or crimson? So often our hopes are dashed just before the winning-post.

We all know the things they like—being kept warm in the winter for one thing. One year I thought I'd be very kind to them, and I put them in a paper bag and hung them in the hot-air cupboard. I didn't look at them until May, when it was time to plant them out, and then to my disgust I found a little mouse had been there first and had left nothing for me.

To give them every chance, a light, well-drained soil is best, in as warm a spot as possible, and they should be kept well-watered when flowering time comes round. Mine increase very fast, and each autumn there are innumerable tiny corms attached to mother; but they do not bloom every year. Sometimes I wonder why I bother to plant them every season, and then when I do get a flower, it is so beautiful and the scent so ravishing that I forget all about the disappointments. Gardening is rather like family life, sometimes very unfair. The difficult children get more fussing and attention than the normal little dears, who give no trouble and cause no heartaches.

~ 5 ~

Primroses

One of the most exciting things about living in the country, to me, is the fact that primroses grow wild. I have lived most of my life near London where a primrose is a cultivated plant, and to find them everywhere, under every hedge and on all the banks, is an excitement that never gets less as the years go by. Early in February they begin to show their pale beauty, but in the shelter of my garden, where they do not have to compete with coarse weeds and rank grass, I often get them before Christmas.

It always amazes me how enthralled collectors get over primroses. I think these modest little flowers create as much excitement as orchids or rare stamps. I know myself that if I want a special one I want it very badly and write round to everyone who may have it. Then I pay a very high price, and ten to one it won't like me and disappears after lingering for a year or so.

I can remember having a terrific campaign to get a small brick- coloured polyanthus called 'Fair Maid'. I heard of it first in an article by Clarence Elliott. Then I read more about it in a book about primroses, and felt I couldn't live without it. I ordered it one autumn from a good nursery, and could hardly wait for the spring to see it in bloom. I watched those plants for the sign of a bud, and when the buds swelled, I climbed down into the ditch at least twice a day to see how they were getting on. I began to have fears when I saw the first glimmer of colour. It was crimson, dark crimson with a hint of magenta, and though I tried hard I couldn't fool myself that it was brick red. When the flowers came out, of course, I knew they were wrong. Every single one was the same, and because the breed was a good doer and I had been busy dividing, there were a lot of them. My little family were all 'Spring Darling', an estimable young person, and I have nothing against her except that she wasn't 'Fair Maid'.

The nursery was apologetic; they said the two kinds were growing side by side, and they would send me 'Fair Maid' to put right the mistake. I didn't get the second batch till the autumn, so I had to go through the agony of waiting for another winter.

Some primroses have distinctive foliage; I can pick out the flat, round leaves of 'Jill' anywhere and the crinkleness of 'Eldorado', but I had never made the acquaintance of 'Fair Maid' and didn't know what I was looking for, so I wasn't prepared for another disappointment—another batch of that hearty, bouncing maiden 'Spring Darling'.

I decided I must try another source; so after much correspondence I got a small plant of 'Fair Maid'. I planted it and cosseted it and waited, but just to spite me it didn't flower next season; then we had our usual spring drought, and the little dear gave up the struggle. I had waited and wasted three years.

By this time the bit was well between my teeth, so I tried another source for my elusive little friend and waited another year. That spring was a bad one, mild to begin with and then exceptionally hard, and a lot of primroses did not flower. So I still had not seen 'Fair Maid'. But one blustery day in early February in my fifth year of waiting, I had one of the great thrills of my life.

A week or so earlier, it being mild and damp, and having a tool in my hand I had divided a very fat clump of primroses. Perfectionists won't agree, but I think conditions are more important than season of the year, and my plants get divided in every month of the year. The label had disappeared from this clump, and I can remember thinking, 'I suppose this will be another of the magenta-mauves, it is such a strapping creature.' But the bud that excited me wasn't crimson but the colour of an old brick wall. It was very full and I wondered if I had somehow hatched a new double. I couldn't wait for it to open properly, but picked it and took it into the house, and with my thumb persuaded it to unfurl those thickly overlapping petals. And then I realized that I had 'Fair Maid' at last—and quite a number of them. I had read about the double eye, which is really a ridge round the centre of the flower; but the neat markings and formation of the bloom are quite unusual and reminded me somewhat of an auricula.

If I had realized what the plant was that I was dividing so recklessly, I should have fussed over it as I have with so many others, and I am pretty certain I should have been disappointed again.

In spite of all I have had to say about 'Fair Maid'—and I can get just as lyrical over many others—I really think of all the primroses and primulas in cultivation the most beautiful of all is the common primrose, *Primula vulgaris.* If it were the most difficult and rare species, we should all get down on our knees and worship it; whereas now I fear we take it very much for granted.

My husband shared my enthusiasm for this lovely flower, which comes so early and bravely defies snow and bitter cold. When we bought the strip of the orchard adjoining ours, he took me out to show me a deep hollow between the trees. 'You might make something of that' was his comment, and went on to suggest primroses and foxgloves and other woodland plants, for which the site was imploring. That was, of course, while we were basking in our daydream of turning our orchard into a garden. I duly planted drifts of natural and coloured primroses in that grassy dell, and some of them have survived to this day, in spite of cows and neglect.

I remember once admiring a bowl of mixed primroses and polyanthus, all rather rare and pedigreed. I identified some and was given the names of others, and when I admired a very pale, pale flower of exquisite charm, expecting to hear it was something exceedingly rare, I was amazed that it was none other than our little woodland friend.

How lovely are our wild primroses studding the banks and verges, and they look just as lovely in our gardens if we give them the same setting. You can have clumps of them under trees and hedges; as a carpet for the dull shrubbery, there is nothing better and little colonies tucked in odd corners and under old walls are spring personified. They grow large and buxom in the good soil of the garden.

I think coloured primroses should be used just as informally. *Primula* Wanda has become a hackneyed horror, spaced between forget-me-nots or tulips in straight rows, to be pecked by birds under the glaring sun. But it is really quite lovely used naturally and inconspicuously. The colour is much more beautiful in the shade, and the flowers are finer. Nor do they seem to offer so much temptation to the birds. I like to see them planted on banks and in shady corners, under trees and shrubs, and in neglected, unexpected places. I plant them in the vertical crevices of my low, supporting walls, and there is nothing more beautiful than a chain of purple flowers peeping out between the stones. I poke them into the crannies at the bottom of the walls, between the stones of the paths. Here they lean back happily against the wall, and make themselves into enormous clumps and cover themselves with flowers.

There are endless coloured primroses. I nearly always find a new one whenever I get a new nurseryman's list, so it is quite impossible to mention them all. But there are some that can't be left out: *P. altaica grandiflora**, for instance, which flowers so early that there are often blooms before Christmas. Its pale pink-lavender flowers are entrancingly clean and gentle in the early spring. I don't think we make enough use of *P. juliae,* the mother of them all, who creeps over the ground and covers territory at a prodigious rate. The leaves are tiny and the delicate little flowers are paler and less outspoken than *P.* 'Wanda', but have a charm of their own. Her white counterpart is even more alluring, but it has a delicate constitution and I find it not too easy to keep. Several new salmon-coloured primroses have come along, but I don't think any of them touch the older 'E. R. Janes', tiny and temperamental though she can be. There are a whole family of Greens, including 'Betty' and 'David', in various shades of velvety crimson; in the mauve and lavender groups we have *P. crispii,* 'Mauve Queen', 'Groeneken's Glory'*, and many others. There are some bright pinks among the old primroses, but they are difficult to find and difficult to keep. I like the more robust 'Kinlough Beauty', sometimes called 'Irish Polly', with its twinkling little pink flowers, edged with silver and finished with an orange eye. My favourite among the purples is 'Jill'. with deep, deep flowers nestling among flat, crinkled leaves. The dark red velvety 'Miss Massey' is the origin of the queen of doubles, 'Mme de Pompadour'*, and 'Craddock White' is still the favourite in the white group, with its long stalks and fine flowers. Some of the other popular kinds are polyanthus in type. 'Lady Greer's' pink flushed cream flowers are bunched, and so are those of 'Dorothy', who is a smaller edition of her Ladyship. Two other good polyanthus types are 'Mrs McGilvray'*, in deep orchid, and 'Crimson Queen', a very good red.

Bronze-leaved primroses have their fascination, although I don't think they are as effective as the green-leaved varieties; the leaves are too much the colour of mother earth to show up well, and my own taste is for a green background for the flowers. There is a whole tribe of 'Garryardes'; 'Victory' and 'Crimson' are the reds, and 'Guinevere', with large pinky lilac flowers. 'Tawny Port' is well described, and there is a smaller one with the same colouring which we all call 'F. Ashby', because it originated with someone of that name.

I have a great liking for green flowers, and a large single green primrose is one of my most cherished plants. It is just like an ordinary primrose, but the flowers are bigger and the leaves longer. Most people say the double green primrose is more interesting than beautiful, but I like it. The only one I know is foliaceous, really the sepals gone wild to produce a double effect, and the one we all want and can't find is the real double flower, with a rosette of petals not sepals.

I am glad that the old double primroses are coming back to favour. The present ones do not seem to have quite the stamina of those of olden days, which flourished with zest in little cottage gardens and in the great walled gardens of the big houses. The double white and double lavender (alba plena* and lilacina plena) are the easiest, and therefore the cheapest, and I think the most beautiful. This may be because they do better than most of the others and therefore look happier. They don't need to be coaxed and cajoled as much as their haughty sisters, and flower more generously. The double lilac used to be called 'Lady's Delight' or 'Quaker's Bonnet*', and I know nothing that excites me more than to see a patch of them in full bloom. I used to think that the paler colours were easier than the deeper ones, but that was before I lost all my 'Bon-Accord Purity'* and most of the pale yellows, 'Sulphur' and 'Cloth of Gold'. Of course the deepest of all is the most difficult, the aristocratic 'Mme de Pompadour'*, who is most difficult to please, and I often wonder how she has managed to survive to this day.

To anyone starting on double primroses I would recommend the double white and double lilac, and either 'Marie Crousse' or 'Bon-Accord Gem'*. The last two are both easy and very much the same colour, although there is a little mauve in the crimson of 'Marie Crousse' and a silver edging to her petals. 'Crathes Crimson' used to like me but doesn't much now; why I can't say, and many of the others come and go in the same way. 'Red Paddy' is a dear little thing, with small, neat flowers, all nicely edged with white, but it can be a little beast and as difficult to please as 'Crimson King', which likes you one day and doesn't the next. I don't think any of the blues are very easy, though some people succeed with 'Marine Blue'. It has a disconcerting way of coming purple when it first starts to flower, and at no time is the blue so true as in 'Bon-Accord Blue'*. The purples are fairly easy, with 'Tyrian Purple' perhaps the easiest. The fabulous one was 'Chevithorne Purple', which used to be a most vigorous and handsome creature, but has dwindled with the years and is now difficult to find and even more difficult to keep when found. 'Our Pat' is a modern one and quite responsive, with bronzed leaves and violet flowers. 'Arthur du Moulin' isn't too reliable, but I pin my faith on 'Downshill Ensign', which has rich purple flowers on rather tall and very upright polyanthus stems. I once had 'Ronald', a pleasant little thing in soft pink and cream, who kept giving me heart attacks by producing occasional single flowers. Pink *juliae* is a fragile plant, with small pale flowers above slender purplish leaves. 'Castlederg' doesn't please me much with its mixture of pink and cream, and 'Curiosity' is just as mad as its name. I have never had it, and it would be only for its rarity and not for its charm that I would cherish it.

I'd like to be able to give an absolutely reliable method for succeeding with double primroses, but I don't believe there is one. Most growers have some preference, which may succeed one year and fail dismally the next. I think the two most important things we can do is to give them shade in very hot weather and keep them moist. I am sure a heavy soil pleases them more than a light one and undoubtedly some humus should be added if possible. The most successful grower I know ploughs rotted chaff into his ground every year, and replants his divisions in a new place each season. I have found changing the site sometimes bucks them up; I am sure they get tired of going on living in the same place year after year.

I grow most of my double primroses in pockets in the bank of the ditch, and use big stones to keep up the earth. The plants that can nestle back against the great stones seem the happiest, so I imagine a little shelter is acceptable. Others that have done well were planted in a piece of ground that used to grow vegetables and which I have now annexed for a small shrub and specimen garden. Here the soil is particularly heavy and there is no sign of all the tons of manure that must have gone into it, but I think it must be there: the primroses seem to know.

There are several schools of thought about the right time to divide primroses. Obviously, the best moment would be directly they have finished flowering, but that is just the time when so often there comes a long, long drought, and unless it is possible to water regularly, I prefer to leave the job until we have a damp spell. I am afraid I divide my primroses at all times, often when I ought to be doing something else, but I find myself tempted to leave my weeding or cutting down if I see a fat clump obviously anxious to be split up—but only if the weather is right.

If you once start collecting primroses, there is no end to it. You certainly want all the hose-in-hose primroses you can find; I know I do. How old they are I don't know, but they must have been grown in 1595, as both Gerard and Parkinson refer to them. Their name dates them, as it undoubtedly originates from the double hose that men wore at that time, the two pairs being put on together, the outer finishing at the knee and the inner reaching to the thigh.

The first hose-in-hose I had was 'Canary Bird'. The two perfect flowers of soft yellow, inside each other, are strangely beautiful, and add a grace and length to the flowers. I have had both the 'Sparklers', but they didn't like me. 'Scottish Sparkler' is bright red with a vivid yellow eye, and the Irish form is larger and sometimes goes by the name of 'Old Vivid'. There is a soft pink, called 'Clarissa', and a hose-in-hose form of our old friend 'Wanda'. In another the petals are candy-striped in pink and red, and we call it 'The Clown'.

'Lady Lettice' is more robust than her elegant Victorian name might lead one to suppose, and has primrose flowers flushed with apricot. In 'Lady Molly' the flowers are rosy lilac, and in 'Dark Beauty' a deep rich crimson. I once had a tiny blue polyanthus hose-in-hose, but it was too precious for this life. I lost 'Lady Dora', too, a tiny cowslip hose-in-hose on a dignified upright stem.

On the whole, I think the other type of primrose, jack-in-the-green or jack-in-the-pulpit, are easier to grow, and certainly just as fascinating. I love the green Tudor ruff in which the flower nestles, made by the sepals which are enlarged to small green leaves. Most of them go just by their colours—mauve, pink, white, brown, or red, but there are a few named varieties. 'Orlando', for instance, is just like an ordinary wild primrose, except for his fleshy green ruff, which gets puffier and puffier as the flowers fade until in time it is so heavy that the slender stem bends under the weight of it. The other yellow one I like is 'Eldorado', a glistening butter yellow with crinkled ruffs. growing in a neat bunch with very large and crinkled foliage. 'Salamander' is the biggest one I know, and has flowers the size of a half- crown on ten-inch stalks. The colour is a glowing red, with a yellow eye, and the green ruff is very important. One called 'Tipperary Purple' is really not purple but a deep mauve, not unlike the colour of 'Wanda's Rival', and it has a small neat way of growing which endears it to me.

Another old primrose that I once had and have no more is Jackanapes, named after the striped Jackanapes coats that the dandies liked to wear in Tudor times. It can't quite make up its mind whether to be a Jack or a hose-in-hose. It has the duplex habit of a hose-in-hose, but the second flower is striped with green and white and has the pleasant habit of persisting long after the self-coloured flowers have withered and gone, so there are really two bloomings. Mine was red, but I believe there is—or was—a very fine pink one.

'Jackanapes on Horseback', or 'Old Franticke', goes even one better and flaunts a little bunch of leaves at the stem junction all gaily splashed with red and white. I have never seen a 'Pantaloon' or a 'Gallygaskin', but I understand the first combines the characteristics of both types, the double flower and the enlarged calyx; while the 'Gallygaskin' is named after the wide hose of the sixteenth century for the enlarged calyx is finished in a frilled ruff below the flower, in the manner of the frilled ruff worn below the knee by the gentlemen of those days.

I expect it is heresy to say that I think breeders are spoiling the charm of polyanthus by making the flowers so very big. I am afraid I really prefer some of the old ones, with their small flowers, very often laced with gold or silver. I have a lovely blue creature with a silver edge to her petals, and a hard-eyed little wench called 'Sceptre', with small neat petals in dusky crimson each completely outlined with pale yellow.

There are two notables in the polyanthus world, away from all the fancy strains that are appearing so often nowadays: one is 'Barrowby Gem', a lovely thing with flowers of palest yellow with a green eye and a most heavenly scent, and 'Bartimeus', the old eyeless primrose. It is so dark a crimson that it looks black in the rain, and is made more intense by the absence of the eye.

I don't expect everyone to agree with me, but I think the polyanthus family are often misused as badly as poor old 'Wanda'. I can't bear to see them set out in rows in the relentless sun instead of being planted in little colonies between taller subjects, which will give them that little bit of shade these woodlanders really need. When I see polyanthus bent over in the heat, I feel there ought to be a society for the protection of flowers as well as children and animals.

Polyanthus are like primroses and must be divided very regularly. In the spacious days of many gardeners this was done as a matter of routine, when the plants were lifted after flowering and replanted for a peaceful summer under a north wall in the kitchen garden. Few of us have time or space for that sort of thing now, and the best we can do is to lift and divide the plants after flowering and put them back in the places where they are to flower next spring. I always feel that polyanthus should be used like primulas, incidentally rather more formally, having little plantings in odd places, under walls and under the shade of trees. I like to keep them in colour groups, and I wish the people responsible for public gardens would do the same; half the beauty of the plants is destroyed when reds, oranges and yellows are all mixed up together.

There is one garden I know where generous beds for polyanthus have been made among the shrubs, and split logs used most appropriately to keep up the soil. Our present style of informal gardening, using many shrubs, offers wonderful opportunities for the good use of polyanthus and all the primula family.

Auriculas seem to be getting back some of their popularity. I am very glad because they are an old-fashioned flower, reminiscent of old prints and sun-bonnets. I think they must have developed temperament during the years, because our forebears had no difficulty in growing them and they flourished in the most ordinary gardens, even in the uninviting atmosphere of the mining villages, for auricula growing was a common hobby of the miners in those days. They don't seem to be so easy to please today, though for some people they do thrive and mutiply. Other equally keen and careful gardeners have great difficulty in keeping them alive. It doesn't seem to be a matter of soil or position. I have seen lovely ones bordering the heavy clay beds in a kitchen garden; another good display was in a series of rocky crevices in full sun; while another lot flourished in a dank little bed against a house with practically no sun at all. And it always seems to me that the people who bother about them least have the best results. I grow mine in deep pockets between stones on a steep south bank, and I try to keep them happy by putting flat stones over their roots. I haven't managed to keep the lovely and rare green ones, but so far most of the others are happy. I think this type of primula likes stones; I know that the smaller varieties—*marginata* and pubescens—do best wedged between stones, and those I grow in stone troughs are always happier with a stone to their backs.

A primula I have grown for a long time and enjoy very much is *P. sieboldii.* I believe it used to be more popular than it is today, judging by the number of varieties listed in old garden books. I was given it years ago by a friend who found it growing in ordinary soil in ordinary beds in a house she bought. She took no trouble with it at all, and it came up year after year, increasing generously and flowering profusely. I have it in three colours—white, mauve and cerise. The white form is the finest and strongest, I think the mauve one the loveliest, and the pink a little too Japanese in colour for me. But I love them all and wish I had more north walls, for I find they do best under a north wall, with plenty of humus in the soil. I think they are quite hardy and I do not know why more people do not grow them. The flowers are in loose sprays on six-inch stalks, and the beautifully cut foliage is a delicate green. They look like greenhouse primulas growing in the cold out of doors, and I feel about them rather as I do about such exotics as incarvilleas and nerines—almost too good to be true.

I started my collection of candelabra primulas with *P. japonica,* which is the easiest and can be grown quite well under a north wall if a really damp spot is not available. I have rather weakened on *P. japonica* now as, with the exception of 'Miller's Crimson', the colours are not too pleasing. The pinks tend to get purplish and mismanage their matrimonial affairs so badly that some of their progeny are as ugly as a piebald cat. I now concentrate on Lissadell and Asthore hybrids, which have a lovely range of colours from salmon pink to deep mauve and never produce a mottled child. *P. pulverulenta* has given me up, too. For years I had lovely Bartley strain primulas, which seeded themselves and came up year after year, and delighted me with their delicate flesh tints, but they disappeared and I haven't tried again. I believe this primula should be sown each year if one wants to keep it, but I prefer the kinds that sow themselves.

The lovely yellow *helodoxa* doesn't like me either, and I imagine it is because I cannot offer it a really wet place. Now I grow *P. prolifera,* another yellow, which seems to forgive the lack of water. *P. florindae* is good-tempered, too, will grow anywhere, and seeds itself well. I expect it would grow bigger in a wetter place, but even with me it makes sturdy eighteen-inch stems topped with mop-heads of hanging primrose bells. It is worth growing for its scent, if for nothing else. I have it in various odd places, and almost forget about it until I am enraptured by a heady perfume and wonder, for a moment, from whence it comes. The so-called red form of *florindae* is more like dirty orange to me, and I do not think it compares with the primrose form.

I try to give *Primula rosea* as damp a place as I can; it has hardly any roots at all, and I am sure needs its nourishment at ground level. I find it one of the most fascinating primulas to grow; first its tight little rosettes of pinkish leaves, then tiny buds of sealing-wax red, which open to intense pink flowers. I think *Primula rosea* in all its forms should be grown by itself, that hard, uncompromising pink doesn't go with anything except white or cream, and it positively screams at the rich yellow of *Lysichiton* (skunk cabbage), which is sometimes planted too near it.

I have had other Asiatic primulas from time to time, but I find I do not keep them. For a season I enjoy the loveliness of *P. chionantha, P. alpicola,* and all the others, and then they disappear, and I haven't taken the trouble to grow on more. One season I had some lovely clumps of *P. vialii,* and all my visitors inquired what new kind of red-hot poker I was growing. But I lost them, alas; so now I stick to a few old favourites, who refuse to leave me and make sure there is another generation each year to carry me through.

~ 6 ~

Irises

An all-the-year-round garden means that there is something in bloom every month of the year, and I know no family of plants that can manage this outstanding feat better than the irises. I have often thought that it would be fun to collect irises; I mean, go to the ends of the earth so that one had every iris that would grow in an ordinary garden, but I don't think I could ever do this because there are so many plants to love, and there wouldn't be room for them all if I filled my garden with the iris tribe. But I think one could collect in a mild way, and be satisfied to have irises in bloom every month in the year, which I believe can be done if one is clever enough.

People have different ideas about growing irises. In a very large garden where there is room for everything, a formal iris garden is delightful, particularly if there is a symmetrical pool and stone paths or coping. But in a small garden I always think it is a pity to coop up all the irises by themselves instead of letting them mingle with the rest of the population. Most people grow only the tall bearded irises, and they all come out at the same time, and when their brief season is over there is a dull patch for the rest of the year.

Another reason why I like to mix them is that they add so much to the rest of the garden. The foliage of the iris is always beautiful, and it is very helpful in a mixed border, even when the irises are not in bloom. And when they are—well, then there is lovely colour to be used just where we need it. Also, I think it is a waste to crowd all the different colours together in a small space. Grown in single clumps in different parts of the garden, I think one enjoys each individual colour more.

I don't expect everyone to agree with me in this mixed gardening idea of mine. People with large gardens usually take an iris garden and a rose garden as a matter of course, and I know that these are the two things for which many a modest gardener yearns.

Sometimes an iris and lupin garden can be very effective. At Barrington Court, in Somerset, there was a garden I liked very much in which irises were grown with phlox and lavender, against a background of fancily cut box trees. That garden was lovely until eel- worms got busy with the phloxes and they had to be removed. Now annuals are used with the irises, and they are quite successful, too, because low ones are used to throw up the silhouette of the irises. That is another of my reasons for not wanting an iris garden—the plants are all the same height and become a mass, instead of each clump being clearly outlined in its beauty and grandeur.

When we talk about irises, most of us mean the tall bearded variety, *germanica,* which bloom in June. It is these that we feature in our iris gardens or mixed borders—according to taste! Lovely as these are, I wouldn't want to limit my iris friends to them alone. For one thing, they flower in high summer when everything else is in bloom, and I like flowers that bloom for me in the winter.

Iris histrioides, for instance, blooms no matter what the weather is doing in January. We may be having snow and ice, the heavens may be deluging us daily with cold winter rain, or there may be bitter north-easters shrivelling up a bleak countryside. No matter what unpleasantness is going on in the air above, the bulbs of *Iris histrioides* that were planted with such care the year before will send up their buds in January, all sheathed in opaque tissue that might well be polythene. And in a few days the flowers will be out, to dazzle and inspire for several weeks. I do not know any blue to equal it (it is azure in its most intense form) and it always makes me think that spring is near, no matter how deep the snow or how strong the wind that whips those fragile blooms till the petals are tattered.

Another winter-flowering species is just as lovely, but not nearly so dependable. The first year I had *Iris danfordiae* in my rock garden it bloomed like a little angel, and I went about telling everybody about the lovely little yellow iris with green finger-marks that blooms in February. I hope my advice wasn't taken by many people because after that it has never deigned to flower for me, I believe because the bulbs divide into tiny ones. Now I plant it in a bowl of peat which I bury under peat and bring indoors when the tips of the flowers are showing. If you have an alpine house, it is a very good place in which to grow it. The finished bulbs go back into the garden, of course.

Iris reticulata, which comes next, gives me no trouble. I rather think it likes my lime soil. I know people with acid soils who complain that it won't flower for them. Part of the charm of this iris is its delicious violet scent. Highbrow gardeners always tell us to go for 'Cantab' as the better form, but that has no scent and the intense blue of its flowers doesn't compensate for that lack. But there are other good variations of *Iris reticulata* in varying shades of violet, plum and purple.

I always get a thrill when I see the first little *Iris pumila* in bloom; I never remember that they bloom so early, and they come before I expect them. I have these little irises everywhere in the garden, in paving and beside my stone paths, tucked into crannies below walls, in pockets in the rock garden, and even in a wall when I can make a place for them. Every year they take me by surprise. One day in early March there'll be a big purple iris head about three inches from the ground, nestling in its pigmy iris foliage. And then there'll soon be a primrose one, and after that blues and yellows, smokey grey and burgundy, and a delicate pink called 'Peach Blossom'. 'Orange King' is scented and blooms a little later than some of the others.

That is one of the nice things about *Iris pumila,* although they begin so early in the year they go on intermittently till May. I remember one year a patch of tiny primrose irises near the garden door was in bloom with forget-me-nots and pale pink arabis, making a lovely colour pattern that I have never managed to achieve again.

The only white *Iris pumila* I know is 'The Bride'*, and she isn't really white; and I doubt if she's really a true *Iris pumila,* as she is taller than the others and flowers later. Her flowers are greeny white and her foliage a little more elegant than the stocky leaves of the other *pumilas.*

*Iris chamaeris** is often taken for a *pumila.* It is a little later than the *pumilas* and slightly taller. Another nice thing about it is the way its foliage keeps good during the winter. In some of the *pumilas* the leaves almost disappear in the winter months.

With my passion for green flowers, I like very much the snake's head iris, correctly known as *Hermodactylus tuberosus.* Many people consider it dull; I admit the flower is small for its stalk. The place to grow it is in a semi-wild part of the garden, if you have such a place, and among plants about the same height. I don't think it minds a little shade; in fact, it is one of those plants you should come on unexpectedly in an odd corner, and because you didn't expect to find anything exciting there, it is a great thrill to meet a patch of these green-and-black flowers, swaying in the breeze.

I have never been very successful with the two little American irises, *I. cristata,* and its little brother, *I. lacustris.* I think I have failed because I have treated them too well. Obviously, such small and precious plants must go in a place where they won't be lost, and obviously, the rock garden is the place for them. But they don't appreciate good living, and very soon cease to take an interest in life. They really like the stony hazard of a gravel path, where they are at the mercy of traffic and weed-killers, but even with such dangers they seem to do better than pampered in the lap of luxury.

Another exciting iris is *I. susiana,* the Mourning Iris, so called because of the fine black marking on its silver-grey face. It flowers in May, too, but not a tiny iris this time but a strapping wench on eighteen-inch stems.

Iris graminea, the grassy iris, comes out about the same time. I often miss the first few blooms of this enchanting plant because the flowers are much shorter than the leaves, and until there are enough to make a good patch of colour, the leaves hide them. As a rule, I prefer my flowers growing and am always loth to pick them, but with *Iris graminea* I have no such qualms. I want to see the exquisite little flowers which are shaded purple blue and plum, and are lightly etched with yellow at the tips of the petals. And even if the flowers themselves were not so beautiful, I'd love them for their delicious scent of greengages—ripe greengages from a sun-baked wall.

There is another form of *Iris graminea,* known as *angustifolia*,* in which the leaves are even more grassy, but it does mean that the flowers show up more and are not shrouded in grassy greenery. If I had a nice low shed somewhere, I think I should have it thatched so that I could grow *Iris tectorum,* the Japanese roof Iris, on it. But all my outbuildings are very tall and very stony, and I don't think the irises would settle in well among tiles even if I could climb up to plant them. So I have had to find another place for these irises. At the back of the malthouse, there is a small brick gully between the wall and the path. My husband had it put there when we made the path, and it was scientifically constructed to take away the water from the roof and prevent it spoiling the precious path, which was then gravelled. After my husband died, I had guttering ('shooting' is the Somerset name for it) put all round the outbuildings, with large cider barrels to catch the water. Now I have four big rainwater barrels at strategic points, so that I never have to go far when I want a can of water. I wish I could do something of the same sort to catch the water from the house. We have the shooting all right, but all that lovely rain-water goes down the drain. It makes me almost ill to hear it gushing away when we have heavy rain. I feel I am losing the lifeblood of the garden, but there is nothing I can do as there is really nowhere to put a barrel.

But to go back to our roof irises: they seem to enjoy living at the bottom of the wall. I filled the gully with a nice planting mixture of loam and lime rubble, and by degrees I am getting the irises all the way along the malthouse. I had only a couple of plants to begin with, but by dividing them every time there is anything to divide, I have got them almost to the end of the building. What happens after that I don't know; I haven't any other place in mind yet. When I feel kindly disposed towards them, I pull off some bits of plaster from the inside wall of the malthouse and scatter the crumblings between them. And when I am scattering wood ash, there is always a dusting for the denizens at the bottom of the wall. I segregate the colours and have blue only in this place. So far I have one or two white ones only.

When we were making the garden, we partially pulled down a wall that divided the barton from the orchard. Now there is a rock garden in front of what is left of the wall, and I am growing white *tectorum* in the remains of the wall. I am not sure that it is the best place because being accustomed to lolling against a cosy thatch, they don't like draughts very much and I am afraid they get them here.

Irises are useful things because they don't need much room. You can poke the dainty little *Iris gracilipes* in anywhere so long as it is shady and moist. It is only nine inches tall and a lovely shade of lilac pink. *Iris innominata* is another May iris, which does best in a sunny position that does not get dry. Again, it is dwarf and neat and in many delightful pastel shades now, not just the butter yellow that used to be the only colour. These irises are very dainty, with faint pencillings, and are said to get annoyed if divided or moved. I know at least one gardener who lifted some and divided them without having them die on his hands as a rebuke, so perhaps they are better natured than some people think.

Of course, June is *the* month for irises, beginning with the earlier and slightly smaller type, *Iris intermedia**. There are some lovely colours in this range: violet, yellow, and blue, and a deep maroon called 'Red Orchid'. An odd clump or two in small borders makes a welcome change from the giants.

There are so many of the big *Iris germanica* that nobody could possibly know them all. And if you did manage to be on bowing terms with most of them, it would not avail you much because the next year there would be many more new ones, and the introducing business would have to start all over again. But we all have our favourites. My favourite white is 'Gudrun', and there is a delicious pink called 'Pink Ruffles'. 'Cleo' has a distinct green tinge about it, but not as green as 'Green Pastures' or the smaller 'Green Spot'. I still grow 'Shot Silk', various good reds, a steely blue, and a very nice pale one called 'Mother of Pearl'. For those who like something strong and definite, I still think 'Ambassador'* is very good, with tones of brown, purple and crimson.

I think irises look particularly good growing in stone, and that is perhaps one reason why formal iris gardens are usually made with stone paths, stone copings and balustrades. I grow my irises among other flowers, and try to get as many of them as I can tight up against the stone paths, so that one gets the full effect of their beautiful swordlike foliage. They do have a very short season, no one can deny it, but I think one can prolong it a little by taking off every dead head every day.

Iris sibirica comes out towards the end of the June display, and the finest flowers are always those growing near water. There is a good range among these irises. I think the white one is the most lovely, but the various shades of blue are good, too, and now we have a new colour in 'Eric the Red', which is really more wine-coloured than red.

If I had a wild garden and if I couldn't find all the seed-pods I want by the roadside, I should most certainly grow *Iris foetidissima*. As a matter of fact, I have several plants, and I am always pulling out seedlings. Why is it, I wonder, that the wild iris like our 'stinking' friend of the hedgerows and the common yellow water iris, *pseudacorus,* seed themselves so embarrassingly and our cherished cultivated irises seldom do. Come to think of it, I can't remember ever finding a seedling of any of my garden irises, but as they increase so satisfactorily, I suppose it doesn't matter.

Those of us who grow our wild friend do so entirely for the seed-pods; the flowers are not at all interesting, although I have a primrose-coloured form which is an improvement on the normal insipid blue. I have several haunts where I can pick as many pods as I want, and I try to go at the exact moment before the pods have opened properly. Brought into the house at this stage, they split very quickly, and one can enjoy those brilliant orange-red berries a long time if they are painted with gum, otherwise they soon fall out. In the open, they fall out almost at once or the birds take them. I don't believe they are poisonous, just smelly. Rumour has it that if you rub the leaves in your hands, they smell like cold beef, hence the name 'roast-beef plant'. Another name is the Gladwin iris; why, I do not know.

After such humble company, we go up in the world to meet one of the most exotic of the iris family. Irises are sometimes called the poor man's orchids, and *Iris japonica* is really like an orchid. The leaves are rather wide and a bright yellowish green and grow in the shape of a fan, but they have a nasty way of becoming tattered and brown at the edges just at the time when those fair and fragile flowers are beginning to open. It spreads by underground stems, and once happy and settled, there is no stopping it. Some people find that it doesn't flower well for them. I think it likes to get into a well-established clump before it even begins to think about flowering, and it likes to bask in the sun with its back to a wall. I grow mine in one of the barton rock gardens, which face south, but I don't get so many flowers as a friend of mine does who grows them under a west wall among shrubs, giving a little protection from bitter winds. 'Ledger's variety' is the best form of *Iris* japonica, and there is another iris closely allied, *I. sintenisii,* which has deeper flowers and seems to control its foliage better.

Some of the most lovely irises come from America. California produced *I. douglasiana;* not unlike *I. sibirica,* with slightly broader leaves and bigger flowers in several shades of purple. I am very fond of *I. versicolor,* which is what I call an informal iris. Its foliage is a pleasant grey-green, and I plant it at the corner of a terraced bed so that it can lean over and furnish pleasantly a strategic space. The flowers are bigger than *I. sibirica* and very elegant in pinky-mauve.

When we come to July, there are not so many irises about, although the *ochroleucas** come along about now. I am always glad to see them because I keep to white and yellow (or silver and gold) in my dining-room, and these statuesque irises are magnificent against my old oak panelling. They are the tallest irises I know and sturdy as well. There are usually three or four flowers on each straight stem, which open one after another so one stalk lasts a long time. 'Snowflake' is the name of the white and yellow beauty, and the all-yellow is 'Queen Victoria'. Although I grow mine in an ordinary bed, I think *Iris ochroleuca** really prefers a damp situation; I am quite certain that *I. chrysographes* does. I have grown 'Margot Holmes' and another red for a long time, but I don't think they enjoyed living in an ordinary flower-bed. Now I have planted them in the wettest part of my ditch, and you really wouldn't recognize the buxom beauties they have become.

I bought my first Japanese irises—*I. kaempferi**—very early in my gardening life. They were to disport themselves on the shores of the Lido, that unfortunate water garden that Walter and I made with such care and which was never in fact a water garden. The water just went soon after we had constructed it, and though one part is always damp, it is not in any way a water garden. It is here that I grow my lovely clematis irises, and they bloom regularly for me year after year after the great June festival. I have never disturbed them, and don't know how they'd react to the yearly divide, which most of my plants have to expect. I have prised off small pieces from the outside to give to covetous friends, and one of these days I promise myself to take them in hand. *Iris laevigata* also grows in the damp part of the ditch in white and rose, and a very good late purple iris, bigger than *I. sibirica,* whose name I cannot discover. I think it is the same as the one in the water gardens at Wisley, at the bottom of the rock garden, and along the stream in the Savill Gardens at Windsor.

There is a little dwarf iris, *I. ruthenica,* that sometimes blooms in September and October. It has flowers at other times as well; in fact, I think it has far more flowers than I know about, those deep purple blooms nestle so deeply in the grassy foliage that it is difficult to see them. I know I miss seeing quite a number of my treasures. It means frequent and careful search to find some of them, and there isn't always the time to spare. I think gardeners should try to keep some time for just looking at their gardens, but I don't suppose they ever will. We have our noses in the earth so much that we don't always see the deficiencies, any more than we enjoy all the pleasant little flowers that open to please us.

Winter flowers are really coming into their own these days, and so *Iris stylosa**—*I. unguicularis* to the purists—is now one of the most popular plants in the garden. The lovely thing about *I. stylosa** is that it blooms when you least expect it. Those of mine that flower first are in the front garden, and sometimes a whole week may go by without my going out there. There may be blooms in late October and early November, but I never look early enough and feel thoroughly ashamed when I find the remains of a lovely bloom which I haven't enjoyed. So many people complain that they don't bloom, and when I see the way they are grown, I am not surprised. In its native Algeria, this iris gets very few of the luxuries of life, except unlimited sunshine.

So a warm place and a poor soil are the main essentials. I plant mine at the bottom of every south wall I can find. As much of the rhizome as possible should be above the soil, but sometimes they have to be buried a little deeper when they are first planted. It is impossible to anchor them with the tough, threadlike roots which is all they have before the white fleshy roots appear. So, to begin with, I plant them slightly deeper than they should be, and uncover the rhizomes when they have taken root. When I find a piece of crumbling plaster detaching itself from the inside wall of the malthouse, I detach it still more and scatter the crumbled remains on top of the soil. *Iris stylosa** treated like this doesn't mind being divided and replanted, preferably just after flowering. And if it is luxuriant foliage only you want, it is very simple to bury them deeply in rich soil in a place where the sun will never penetrate.

I used to think there was just *Iris stylosa** like that, but as in so many species, directly you become interested, you discover how many different members there are to each family. My second discovery was the white form of the ordinary *stylosa**, with deep yellow markings. Then I was given *I. speciosus**, which is much deeper in colour and has wider petals with a slightly ruffled edge. There is a white counterpart of *speciosus**. One of the loveliest *stylosas** I know is very pale in colour, and is known affectionately as 'Mr Butt's *stylosa'** because it came from his garden. There is a very rare one with bright blue flowers, and a deeper form of the ordinary variety. In the Oxford Botanic Garden there is a dark, almost striped form, with deeper colours merging into the background. There are two tiny ones called *angustifolia**, with normal-sized flowers and very narrow, grassy foliage. They flower in spring. I have no doubt there are many others, and I hope to meet them one day.

You don't see the scorpion iris, *I. alata**, very often, perhaps because it flowers in December. It is quite hardy, but its pale flowers are too fragile for winter wind and mud. It would probably succeed well in a very sheltered spot and with a good groundcover, like *Arenaria balearica* or *Mentha requienii,* to prevent the lashing rain throwing up mud to sully its pale beauty; but undoubtedly it is safer in an alpine house. *Iris vartani* also needs a sheltered corner if its slate-grey or white flowers are not to be spoiled by the elements. If I had an alpine house, it would be one of my first inhabitants, but as I haven't, I grow it in a bowl of fibre in my living-room, and plant the bulbs outside after they have had their day.

~ 7 ~

Geraniums

By geraniums, of course, I mean the hardy herbaceous plants sometimes known as cranesbills. The tender pot plants so beloved of our Victorian grandmothers are, of course, pelargoniums, and for anyone who has a greenhouse where they can be wintered, there is nothing better for giving colour over a very long period. The people responsible for park bedding know something when they use pelargoniums, and even the most ardent hardy plantists find that there is nothing that takes their place for such important places as beds round the house or in urns or vases.

I have no greenhouse and though I find a few plants of deep pink, double pelargoniums and the paler ivy-leaved trailers are most useful for giving all-the-season colour under the malthouse windows, I have to start each season afresh as I have no way of taking care of the plants in the winter.

But I make no complaint, because I have a very large collection of hardy geraniums in different parts of the garden, and find them a most adaptable and generous family. Many of them flower throughout the season, they fit in anywhere, and in many cases good foliage is another recommendation.

One of the biggest is the tall blue *G. ibericum*. When I see a large clump in full bloom, I think what a wonderful plant it is and wonder why we don't use it more. But it does get a little out of hand after it has flowered, and I think is better among shrubs or in a wildish garden. It blooms in midsummer, and in a good season will start all over again in late October, but I would not call it an intermittent bloomer, like so many of the geraniums.

I wouldn't plant *Geranium ibericum* in a mixed border, although it looks so right in a cottage garden. To me, it is a plant for a semi-wild place, or for odd corners such as are found in the big old gardens near the sheds or stables. In my youth, there were discreet shrubberies that hid the way to the disgraceful back door, and it is in their present-day equivalent that I'd plant it. I love it dearly when it is a sheet of rich blue, and wonder why I don't use more of it; but once it has finished its first flowering and gets big and untidy, I want to dig it up and give it away.

But I would not part with a scrap of *Geranium grandiflorum alpinum**, particularly the variety known as 'Gravetye'*. It is seldom more than a foot high, and is nearly always in bloom. It has neat, graceful foliage, and doesn't seem to mind if it is in sun or shade. I have a crab-apple tree in one of my terraced beds, and I grow this geranium all round that because it looks well when the tree is bare, and there are not many plants that remain neat and well-behaved when most of the time they are under a canopy of leaves. This is the kind of plant I would use if I had a formal border in front of a shrub border and wanted plants that would merge formality happily with informality. The flowers are large, powder blue, veined with pink.

I often wish I had a shrub border or a wild garden in which I could grow more of these pleasant informal geraniums. I put a clump here and there in my ditch garden, but there is not room for them all. There is *G. striatum**, for instance, two feet tall with pale pink flowers, veined with crimson, and with crimson blotches on the neat foliage. *G. viscosissimum* is very much like it, but it grows to three feet instead of two, and its flowers are a deeper colour, although they have the same crimson veins. *G. sylvaticum roseum* is tall, too, and though the flowers are described as *roseum* they have a distinct purple tinge. *Geranium anemonifolium** is considered by some people to be not quite hardy, although I treat her just as I would any other of the woodland type of geranium. I knew one gardener who was so fearful of her safety that he kept her in a pot in the greenhouse. She makes a good three- to four-foot bush with me and is as wide as she is tall, and I often wonder to what proportions she expanded in her rarified home. She is a single-stemmed plant with pale pink flowers in corymbs. There is another form called *G. hirsuta,* with slightly hairy leaves. I have seen this geranium trained against a wall, but whether it is to see how tall she will grow or to give her a little protection, I do not know. The leaves are rather like those of a glorified herb Robert; in fact, I have often nearly uprooted some of her numerous progeny, thinking they were the children of this flower of the wild.

My favourite of all the tall geraniums is the sun-loving *G. armenum** or *G. psilostemon,* as I believe we have to call her now, and it is the only one of the kind that I grow in my terrace garden. I only wish it would increase at the speed of some of the others. I love it at every stage of the game, from the moment it puts its little pink nose through the soil until it opens its wicked eyes. Those black-centred crude magenta flowers would be sinister if they didn't grow gracefully above the most elegant cut foliage, rich in autumn tints.

The most useful of all geraniums is, I think, *Geranium endressii,* in her various forms. The variety 'Wargrave'* is most in demand, with bigger salmon-pink flowers over greyish foliage, but for continuous blooming and generous co-operation in ground covering, I think the ordinary variety is the best. 'A. T. Johnson'* is rather more bushy, but its small dancing flowers are a delicious shade of silvery pink. 'Rose Clair'* is white, with purple veining, very distinct and pretty, and I like one clump of it in the garden, not over and over again as I have the ordinary form of *endressii*.

When I first made my terraced garden, I felt I should be rather formal on each side of the central path. There were cypress trees on each side, *Chamaecyparis lawsoniana fletcheri**, as correct as a Noah's Ark garden, and I made a symmetrical planting. 'Dresden China' daisies made a band against the stones that edged the path; then came *Nepeta mussinii**, with clumps of *Oxalis floribunda** and *Geranium endressii*, and *Viola* 'Iden Gem' behind, giving me colour throughout the season. The geranium makes a heavy mat in a very short time; it is low-growing and persistent. Another place where I found it useful was on the steep bank above the Lido. Those were the two places where I put it; now it plants itself wherever it likes to be. I find it coming out from under trees, and occasionally there will be a swirl growing in a wall. It anchors itself in the tiniest crack in the paving, and covers the surrounding stone with a great mat of soft green foliage and gay pink flowers. It is the easiest plant to increase or decrease, and it is always a lady. I wonder why the experts are scornful about *Geranium endressii* and insist on the superior 'Wargrave'* form. I don't see a lot of difference, and I grow both. The flowers of 'Wargrave'* may be a little bigger, but I don't think there are so many of them as in the commoner type.

It is curious how sometimes one is taken in by the most ordinary flowers. I was staying at Lynmouth with some cousins recently, and we were wandering through a little village nearby, peering through hedges and over gates, as is our custom. We literally hung over one gate to admire some paving in what was obviously a very new garden, and conjectured what could be the lovely pink geranium that was growing in it and along a bed beside the path. We thought it must be something very unusual, so large and bright were the flowers, growing in a very determined, sprightly way. We talked about it all the way back to the hotel, and I thought about it so much that when I got home, I telephoned the village post office to find out who had made that charming little garden. When I got the name, I wrote and asked not only for the name of our mysterious plant but also for a bit of it, and offered anything she liked from my garden. You know the answer, of course—none other than *Geranium endressii*.

The *macrorrhizum* family try hard to be as popular as *G. endressii*. I find them seeding themselves all over the place, and although I love their scented foliage, which tints so beautifully in the autumn, their season of blooming is limited. I first met this geranium making a handsome carpet under an evergreen oak, and I liked the unusual rosy-purple of its flowers. Then I made the acquaintance of the pink-flowered form. There are two pink ones, a rather washy pink and 'Ingwersen's'* variety, which has larger, clearer coloured flowers. I know the last named is held by the experts to be the pride of the race, but I put my money on the white form. Though the flowers are white, their calyces and stems are bright red, which makes it different from any other plant I know.

I grow the white *Geranium phaeum* at the shady end of the Lido bank. It is quite a pleasant little soul, with a succession of small white flowers. The dark form has many names. Sometimes it is called 'mourning widow', but more often the 'dusky cranesbill', for its rather small flowers are such a deep dusky purple as to be almost black. It has a neat habit and nice foliage, and will grow quite happily in shade. *Geranium reflexum* is not unlike it, except that it makes a much bigger plant with larger leaves, on each of which there is a distinct dark blotch.

I think a very good place in which to grow these rather leafy geraniums is under old and species roses. Most of the roses are rather tall and skinny about the legs so that good foliage plants which have flowers that do not compete make a pleasant carpet for them.

I know of only one bulbous geranium, *G. atlanticum**. It has the disconcerting habit of going below ground after flowering and one fears it is lost, but it pops up again in late autumn, nice neat little plants about nine inches high with pleasant leaves and brilliant blue flbwers which are by no means small.

I love to see the wild *Geranium pratense* growing in long grass by the side of the road, and I wouldn't mind one or two plants in my garden if it would leave it at that, but it doesn't, and really becomes a nuisance with its indiscriminate seeding. It has, however, one or two refined relations. 'A. T. Johnson'* is dwarf and sturdy and has flowers of good blue. There is a pink form with flowers most delicately veined. *G. pratense* 'Silver Queen' is a lovely pearly-grey tint with black anthers, and it blooms longer than the rest of the family. The old favourite double blue has been known, I believe, since 1770, and is now coming back into high favour. It goes on blooming for nearly two months, and has flowers of a lovely mauvy-blue.

I can't say I love the common form *Geranium sanguineum* much, although it is the most generous member of the family when it comes to flowers; it is never without a few blooms. 'Once get a foothold in a garden, never give way' is its motto, and I defy anyone to move it when once it has taken hold. It is nearly as bad as *Lychnis flos-Jovis.* When I had very little to adorn my garden, I planted bits of this geranium here and there, and there and here it remains and nothing will ever eradicate it. The white edition is not nearly so possessive, but on the other hand it sticks to union rules when it comes to flowering. Of course the refined form *G. sanguineum lancastriense** is a perfect lady and you find her in the most exclusive rock gardens. There is an even better form, *G. sanguineum grandiflorum**, more compact and low-growing with bigger, deeper pink flowers.

Geranium renardii is a plant some people like very much and others simply can't abide. I am in the first category. Its grey-green leaves are downy and beautifully fashioned, and fine black pencillings on the white flowers make them look almost grey, too. I think this is a geranium that should never be allowed to get too big. When that happens, there are too few flowers for the foliage and it can look almost coarse, but split it up regularly into small clumps and it is never dull.

I am very fond of the two trailing geraniums, and the fact that they both trail is the only thing they have in common. G. traversii 'Russell Prichard'* simply smothers itself in a swirl of silvery leaves and has a magnificent succession of bright magenta-pink flowers all through the summer and autumn. G. wallichianum 'Buxton's Blue' likes to wander long distances from its single-stem root, and is not very easy to propagate. Rather hairy leaves, pleasantly tinted and marked, are sparsely spaced on the long stems, and the flowers are not very big but of such a lovely clear blue that it is not a plant you pass by. I first saw it growing among rocks in a nursery in Worcestershire, and felt I couldn't live without it; and now I don't have to!

There are a few small members of the family, such as G. farreri (syn. napuligerum*), with pink flowers, and staplianum roseum*, pink again and with a pleasant late-flowering habit. G. pylzowianum has pink flowers and silver leaves and blooms from June to September. G. cinereum is another tiny species with grey-green leaves and pale pink flowers. G. cinereum subcaulescens* is a striking plant with intense magenta flowers each with a black eye. G. dalmaticum is a newcomer and grows a little bigger, about nine inches when it gets going well. It makes a nice hummock of round shiny green leaves and pink flowers an inch' across. There is a very pleasant white form, and both increase quite rapidly underground.

I hope someone will some time write a book about geraniums. I find them a very pleasant family to know, and I wouldn't like to be without any of them in my garden.

~ 8 ~

Penstemons

I have written about penstemons before, so perhaps I ought to leave them out of this book, but I don't see how I can write about an all-the-year garden without some reference to plants which I think solve the problem of permanent colour better than anything else.

Penstemons are still regarded by many people as not quite hardy. I don't know how they fare in the North of England, but I know gardens near London where they go through the hardest winters without turning a hair, and, I need hardly say, they are quite reliable with me. But if one has doubts, it is the easiest thing in the world to take cuttings. I fill a large frame every year with penstemon cuttings, for other people mostly. I usually do the main job in the late autumn, but they seem to root quite well any time. I am always adding to my penstemon collection, and never refuse the offer of a cutting whatever time of year it is. I put these odd cuttings in a small frame filled with sand, peat and loam, and they root very quickly. For easy handling, I put those I do on a wholesale scale in boxes and put the boxes in the frame.

If I were responsible for a big garden or park with bedding to do and had plenty of labour, I think I should use new little plants each year. For one thing, they would all be the same size, and for another I think one can hang on to one's old plants too long. I know I do from sheer sentimentality. It seems ungrateful to throw out old friends just because of their age and after they have served one well. The flowers don't seem to deteriorate, and though the plants get bigger each year I don't think one should discard them for that—unless, of course, they are in a place where a big plant is not wanted. I have to harden my heart and do it sometimes, but I still don't like throwing plants away, and always find a good home for them if I can.

I first bought *P. campanulatus* 'Evelyn'* to grow on a rock garden, and my original plant is still there. It doesn't increase as fast as some of them, and I find by cutting it down to ground level in early April I can keep it compact and shapely. I have, of course, many more plants of this lovely little shell-pink penstemon now. They provide colour for six months in the year, and if I have odd corners in the front of my beds and odd cuttings in hand, I put in penstemons.

P. 'Evelyn'* never seeds herself for me, but 'Rose Queen', another of the *campanulatus* group with notched leaves, does. This is a much smaller plant, with smaller leaves and tiny crimson flowers. I am always rooting up little strays and returning them to their mothers, where I think they ought to be.

P. 'Garnet'* doesn't seed either, but it increases rapidly; in fact, I often wish some of my older clumps would feel that they had had enough of this world and let me start again with young stock. I love the glowing crimson of 'Garnet'*, especially with the sun behind it, and have often thought that no plant in the garden is better named. It must be cut down each year if it is to have a semblance of shape and proportion. I know gardens where 'Garnet'* is left alone to do as it will, and believe me, it does a lot. Left to itself, it will grow to four feet and an untidy four feet at that. The stems aren't really strong enough to support much weight; it gets broken and untidy in the wind, and far too diffuse for proper deheading. My plants may be big, but they grow up more or less the same height and deheading them is quite a simple operation.

I used to be positively scared to cut down my penstemon until all danger of frost was over, and left them in their untidiness until the end of March and early April. But lately I have been experimenting, and have come to the conclusion that it really depends on the penstemon. Some of them make a thick growth of bushy foliage near the ground, and I think it is quite safe to take off the flowering stems when there is this carpet of growth below. Penstemon 'Garnet'* grows like this, I am glad to say, and so I can neaten them up for the winter. Others that work in the same way are the tall opalescent 'Stapleford Gem', and a rather small one, 'Purple Bedder'. Sometimes I can do it with 'Hewell's Pink Bedder' and the crimson 'Newbury Gem', but not always.

Some I wouldn't dare to touch. I am a little respectful of 'Evelyn'*, as I don't know how she'd react; as for P. heterophyllus 'True Blue'*, I leave her severely alone, as even without any familiarity she is quite capable of showing displeasure and dying off without any excuse. I don't know whether it is a weak constitution that causes this or a mild dislike of lime. I know that the best ones I ever saw were in the gardens of Mulgrave Castle in Yorkshire, where there is no lime in the soil. I am sure it is safest to keep this temperamental beauty going with cuttings every year. The bigger, blowsier P. heterophyllus, which has a low spreading habit, doesn't make ground-level foliage, but it does cover a large area with a crisscross of stems. I seldom do more than tidy it up in the autumn; it keeps on most of its dark, almost purple leaves, and is quite presentable all through the winter months. It is a good plant for covering the ground and giving continuous colour.

We all have our favourites among the flowers, and I think my favourite penstemon is undoubtedly 'Hewell's Pink Bedder'. I have seen it in catalogues grouped under the hartwegii family. I believe that the hartwegiis are the mother and father of all penstemons, and this may be all that it means. It is certainly an easier plant to use than the scarlet P. hartwegii, which is rather skinny in growth and keeps up that characteristic with its long, tubular scarlet flowers. There is another of the same build with flowers of creamy white, which I think must undoubtedly be the white form. My beloved 'Hewell's Pink' is much more branching; in fact, it is the only really branching penstemon I know. It grows sideways, and evenly so that it makes a nice solid mass of leafage with relay after relay of shrimp-pink flowers. The bells aren't as big as the herbaceous penstemon, but they are bigger than 'Garnet'* and fuller than *hartwegii*.

I have five red penstemons I grow extensively, and I like them all. The smallest is 'Myddleton Gem', which is carmine and has a white throat, and rather like a miniature *P.* 'Castle Forbes'. 'Newbury Gem' is rather small, too, and is crimson with deeper etchings in its throat. 'George Elrick' is rather lighter in tone with the same type of markings. *P.* 'Southgate Gem' is, I think, the most popular in this group. It has larger bells of intense scarlet, but I find it rather difficult to place. It has rather a loose way of throwing its arms about, and really needs to be grown with taller plants round it to keep it straight and firm. I have it with a background of *Lysimachia clethroides* in one place, and it works well. On the other hand, *P.* 'Castle Forbes' stands up proudly and makes a good clump, with fat flower spikes well proportioned to the foliage below. I like the crimson of its big bells and the clear white throats of the flowers.

The two blues I like best are *P.* 'Stapleford Gem' and 'Alice Hindley'. I used to call 'Stapleford Gem' 'Moonstone' before I discovered its real name. That gives you a clue to its colour. It has the same opalescent quality as Purple Bedder but on paler lines, and the spikes of rather small flowers are short in proportion to the big leafy bush that it makes. Now, 'Alice Hindley' I'd call a rangy thoroughbred, a shootin', huntin' and fishin' woman, who is elegant in a raw-boned way. There is nothing smug or self-effacing about her. Up go her spikes of soft blue and white flowers to three and four feet, and she has to be planted among tall plants or given artificial support. I like to see her peering up through a tree mallow to see if the mallow will out-flower her. She needn't worry, the mallow knows its place and that its purpose in life is to be a background.

The 'Hon. Edith Gibbs' is a lovely plant, by no means robust and inclined to send up odd shoots instead of making a solid bush. The flowers are pink—tipped cream and quite large. It never thinks of making new ground growth till the spring, so it never gets touched till then, but it is one of the big-belled type that can be divided. There are usually incipient roots showing on the lower parts of its stems, and all that is necessary is to pull pieces off with a bit of root and there is a new plant. I have done it, but I prefer the nice little plants that come from cuttings.

I don't know in which class I should put *P. isophyllus;* it doesn't fit in anywhere.

It has tall stems with small coral flowers and grey-green leaves which really need a wall as background, and I always find a wall for it. One I have grows at the top of the rock garden near the barton gate, and I have *Veronica hulkeana** in front—two rather special plants together. I think the penstemon is hardy enough, it is only that its long back needs support. *Veronica hulkeana*,* of course, is definitely tender, that is why I plant it in the most sheltered spot I have, with a southern aspect and a wall behind. The bright shiny foliage and long sprays of grey-blue flowers make a good foil for the coral and grey of the penstemon.

My penstemons come and go. There is a beautiful claret one that has exceptionally big bells, and sometimes I have it and sometimes I find it has disappeared and I have to start again. I have never discovered if it is slightly tender or if I am too demanding in stripping it of cuttings. Not long ago I was given a new white one which, I am told by experts, is 'White Bedder', although there is a touch of pink on the cream flowers. They are an unusual shape, rather wide and flaring with prominent stamens.

I think there must be an enormous number of different penstemons grown throughout the country. I get a few new ones every year and sometimes wonder if I have too many penstemons in the garden. But when I am aiming at a garden in which there is colour every month in the year, I don't think I can have too many penstemons.

~ 9 ~

They go on Blooming

I still feel, as I did when I first planted my garden, that it is essential to include quite a number of plants that have a long season of blooming. We want the garden to look nice all the time without dull moments when there are no flowers in bloom, and however skilfully we plan a succession of colour from the short season plants, I don't believe we can manage this without some of the good-tempered plants that are almost always in bloom.

We can't do without all the lovely things that come and go—delphiniums, lupins, irises and poppies—and we welcome them for their brief but spectacular season. If we are clever, we may coax them into a precious second blooming, but in between it is nice to meet old friends who have no office hours and feel that their job is to go on producing flowers so long as the sun shines and there is a vestige of warmth in the air. The plants that oblige in this way aren't always the most spectacular; nor are they, perhaps, the most exalted, but they definitely fulfil a purpose in life. In my idea of a perfect garden, there must always be something to catch the eye and keep up interest, and for this we need the handmaidens as well as the stars.

I put nepeta very high on my list of continual bloomers, nepeta in all its varieties. *Nepeta mussinii** is the one we usually see, and I think it is still the best for most purposes. I have another not unlike it, *Dracocephalum sibiricum** with a flatter habit of growth, larger blue- grey leaves and very pretty lavender flowers. N. 'Six Hills' needs a lot of room, but when there is space I think it is the most showy.

All these nepetas cover a lot of ground though the actual root is very small. When I first started gardening, I used to plant nepeta bang in the middle of a bed, not realizing that I was wasting a lot of space thereby. Now I put it at the edge of a stone path, so that at least half the plant spills over the path, or I wedge it in a wall or between stones at the top of a wall. In doing this, it takes up the minimum of space and leaves room for the other plants that are needed to give colour and interest all the rest of the year.

Nepeta nervosa doesn't sprawl, but both it and 'Souvenir d'Andre Chaudron'* are inclined to wander a little. A narrow bed or an odd crevice are really the best places for them, where they can't get up to much mischief. I have heard suggestions about their complete hardiness, but I have never found them the least bit tender.

Conifers and evergreen shrubs are a crucial element in the winter scene.

The green flowers of *Helleborus argutifolius* are always a winter favourite at East Lambrook.
Previous page: Skimmias dripping with long-lasting scarlet berries bring sparkling colour to an
East Lambrook winter.

These plum-speckled Orientalis Hybrid hellebores still make fat clumps in the garden.

The white form of *Crocus tommasinianus* flowers early but is tough and dependable.

The pink flowers and silvery marbled foliage of *Cyclamen hederifolium* appear in autumn all over the garden.

The genuine 'Betty Green' primrose with its neatly thrum-eyed, velvet crimson flowers.

Primroses self-sow freely in the garden, intercrossing to create a wide range of colour combinations and forms.

"Hen and Chickens" double daisies, here with Mrs Fish's original label marked "H&C"

Geranium x *oxonianum* 'Wargrave Pink' makes fine ground cover but can smother more choice treasures.

Top: *Prunella grandiflora* 'Loveliness' is a neat
and dependable perennial.
Left: *Persicaria affinis*, once known as a
polygonum, is an invaluable low ground cover
for late summer and autumn.

Senecio cineraria 'Ramparts' is a rare, bold form of this very effective silver-leaved species.

Artemisia absinthium 'Lambrook Silver' is one of the classic silver foliage plants and was raised at East Lambrook.

Senecio cineraria 'White Diamond' growing in front of the rich foliage of purple orach, *Atriplex hortensis* var. *rubra*.

The colour in the flowers of *Geranium* 'Johnson Blue' is reflected in the blue-tinted foliage of the flag irises.

East Lambrook Garden in early autumn with perennial asters at the peak of their colour.

The glossy, evergreen foliage of this free-standing *Magnolia grandiflora* 'Exmouth' shines in the winter sun.

'Norah Leigh' is a dramatic variegated form of the old border phlox 'Border Gem'
Next page: *Geranium* x *oxonianum* 'Winscombe' tumbling round an old sink planted with alpines.

Potentillas don't seem to have any set times for blooming, and the commoner they are, the more continuously do they give their flowers. I get rather annoyed with the yellow-flowered *P. recta* when I find its progeny turning up in all sorts of unwanted places, but I must admit that it is a generous giver. Now I have acquired a lemon-coloured version of this plant, and I am encouraging that and being less kindly disposed to the one with deeper yellow flowers. This *potentilla* is useful because of its upright habit of growth. Quite a big sheaf of flowers comes from a very neat tuft of hairy leaves.

Some of the low-growing *potentillas* bloom on and off the whole season. 'Roxana'* in rich brick red, 'Miss Willmott'* in pink with a dark eye, and 'Gibson's Scarlet' with plenty of bright green leaves to make a background for its brilliant flowers. These *potentillas* can be coaxed into any space that is available. If it is bare ground we want to cover, they can be allowed to sprawl and wander to their heart's content, but if there isn't much room, they can be staked to give a concentrated splash of colour between taller perennials.

I plant the big *potentilla* 'Mount Etna'*, with dark smouldering flowers, and silver-lined leaves next to Oriental poppies. I love these poppies, but they are the untidiest things to deal with after they have flowered, and I think the only thing to do is to cut them down, leaves and all, and train *potentillas* or something of the same kind over the unsightly gap. When the poppies make their fresh growth, the *potentillas* can be raised and staked to take their place between them.

There is a good small *potentilla* that blooms early and late and never ramps. *P. tonguei* is good enough for a most select rock garden, and I find it useful to plant at the front of flower-beds and at the edge of stone paths. It is soft orange in colour with deeper markings. I think there are two forms of *Potentilla montana*. The one I have had for a long time and grow where I want a neat-habited, evergreen trailer, has leaves like a diminutive strawberry and a succession of small white flowers in summer and winter. Another I was given recently has narrow, pale green leaves, and is neither so energetic nor densely foliaged. Both *potentillas* will grow among stones quite happily and I never waste on them the valuable space of a front-line bed.

There are two members of the oxalis family that are always in flower. Again, they are distinctly commoners but good value in the first place. One of the first plants I noticed when we came to Somerset was *Oxalis floribunda**. The villagers call it shamrock and give it a place of honour in their little gardens. I did the same when I first planted my terraced garden, which as I said before ought to have rather a formal planting between the little cypress trees that edged the winding path, and chose one that I thought would give colour and interest throughout the season, no matter what the flowers in the rest of the garden were doing. Close against the stones, there was a thick band of 'Dresden China' daisies, then came the soft blue of nepeta merging into the strong pink of *Oxalis floribunda**. The space between the oxalis and the shrubs and perennial plants in the borders was filled with *Viola* 'Iden Gem', a faithful little friend who produces a succession of rich violet flowers winter and summer alike.

I still grow all these plants at the edge of my central path, but not in the same order. 'Dresden China' daisies still pack the crevices between the stones, because they do best when their roots can explore the cool depths between stones. I enjoy my little daisies, but I don't rely on them for much colour as I do on my fat *Bellis perennis,* which bloom on and off all the time. There are usually odd blooms of 'Dresden China' to be seen before and after the great spring display; they practically pack up in the summer, which tries them if it is a very dry one, but damp autumn days see them waxing plump and green again, with odd flowers here and there.

Nepeta, I think, should only be grown in a flower-bed if one has too much room and too few plants. That was my condition when I first planted my terraced garden. Twenty years of extensive collecting has reversed that position, and now I haven't enough room for all the exciting things I want to grow and nepeta has had to give up its comfortable open bed for less luxurious quarters between stones and in odd cracks and crannies in the walls. *Oxalis floribunda**, too, is too easily pleased for such easy living, and has been squeezed into tiny holes at the bottom of walls and even offered a bare subsistence at the edge of the gravel path. I find weeds are inclined to grow too well round the stones that edge the barton, and here I am seconding my poor oxalis. I don't think it will mind, and I am sure it will continue to produce relays of bright pink flowers to open whenever the sun shines.

Oxalis valdiviensis is good-tempered in a different way. It sows itself with casual abandon, and when once it has been invited into a garden, it sees that it is always represented there. It likes to grow in walls and rather hot places, and reminds me somewhat of *Corydalis lutea,* which is just as persistent and impossible to snub. Both plants have the same transparent, brittle stems with small roots which manage to take hold in the tiniest crevice. *O. valdiviensis* has corymbs of yellow flowers on four-inch stalks and a neat, upright habit of growth, different from the rather floppy prodigality of *Oxalis fioribunda.*

I like the new *erigerons* with their big flowers in exciting new colours, but they haven't the long-flowering qualities of some of the old ones. I am fond of 'Elsie', although I have heard complaints that grown in a mass she doesn't show up very well. I don't grow her like that, but put her at the edge of a wall or in a crevice in paving where she can lie back comfortably and send out her long horizontal stems, each tipped with a succession of soft pink flowers. *E. philadelphicus* increases well, and it seeds itself, too. But best of all it will go on flowering into December. I like its small pink flowers, which hang their heads until they open, but to get an effect, I think they should be planted in close formation. I leave the odd plants that seed themselves in paths and walls if they are not doing harm to anyone else.

Erigeron 'Mesa Grande' keeps sending up fresh shoots from ground level, each topped with nice lavender flowers, and so does 'Mrs Beale'* and *azureus*. Perry's variety of 'Mesa Grande' is a deeper and a better colour, but it restricts itself to one flowering, so I merely cut off its heads only to begin with and leave the foliage until it starts to get untidy.

Erigeron glaucus and *Erigeron* 'Elstead Rose'* are alike in growth and alike that they flower on and off all the season. The ordinary type of *E. glaucus* is very dull as to flowers, although it makes a neat clump of green rosettes and fits into any rock crevice that may need garnishing. There are better forms to be had, and I stick to these and have said good-bye to the pale mauve form which is sometimes known as a rock aster. I put *E.* 'Elstead Rose'* in an ordinary flower-bed, but I think it would be very happy among stones as well.

Some people don't like heleniums. My husband didn't. For some reason, he was irritated by those downward sloping petals and said the flowers always looked as though they were fading. I didn't allow him to banish all my heleniums from the garden because two in particular have this pleasant habit of continuous flowering. Most of the tall ones, and such varieties as 'Mine Canivet' and 'Chipperfield Orange', seldom flower more than once, but two very old friends go on all through the year. *H.* 'Crimson Beauty' and *H. pumilo magnifico** were two of the first herbaceous plants I was given, and I have kept them going ever since by constant division. I should like a penny for every one I have given away, but I am sure this is the way to keep them manageable. Let them get big and old and they get woody and the flowers small, but with a succession of fresh growth and tender roots you have good, healthy plants. The yellow of *H. pumilo magnifico** is clear and strong but not aggressive. There is a certain amount of brown in the tones of 'Crimson Beauty' and the dark centres get almost black as they die off. Both are that useful height of about a foot.

I wish *tradescantia* wasn't such an untidy creature. There are nearly always flowers on her among the tangle of foliage, buds and finished flowers. And the flowers themselves are really beautiful, in white and pale blue, deep blue and cerise, but I don't think we get the full benefit of them with such a messy background.

Lamium maculatum is one of the easiest plants to please, its grey and white foliage is always good, and it flowers continually, so for a place that merely needs clothing, I use it very often. I can't say I care much for the magenta-ish pink of the flowers, and I am trying to get enough of the white-flowered form and the one with shell-pink flowers so that I can have them in more places and put my old dull friend in the background.

Agrostemma is not a social highlight, but it has all the qualities of good breeding, so I cherish the seedlings I find everywhere and plant them in odd corners and unimportant beds where something is needed, but nothing very superior. The neat silver rosettes would be welcome even before the rigid grey flower stems start growing and branching, with an unending supply of flowers at the end of each. The one that does best, of course, is the common one and its proper name is *Lychnis coronaria* 'Abbotswood Rose'*, with vivid magenta-rose flowers, called most euphemistically by most nurserymen 'crimson'. There is a deeper coloured one, *L. c. atrosanguinea*, a white-flowered form, and a delightful pale pink one. But the seedlings I find are all magenta!

I have long grown *Campanula persicifolia* in the garden. I don't remember when I got my first plants. I know I bought the blue 'Telham Beauty' and a 'white cup and saucer', but I have a great affection for the ordinary single ones that bloom on and off from June till November. They aren't the most superior, of course, but they seed themselves in good places, like the edge of a wall or the side of a path and send up a succession of lovely blue or white flowers. *C. lactiflora* and *C. lactiflora macrantha* usually bloom only once, but there are three others that are never out of flowers. *C. burgaltii** and *C. van houttei** have large hanging bells in a slaty blue, and *C. alliariifolia (cordifolia*)* goes on producing its tall spikes hung with ivory bells all through the summer. The old cottage garden campanula, *C. latiloba,* is another that keeps sending up fresh flower shoots in various shades of blue and white.

I try not to swamp the garden with yellow, as too much yellow can be overpowering, but I always have a few clumps of *Calceolaria integrifolia*. It makes a nice compact plant about two feet high, and there is plenty of foliage to tone down the yellow flowers. It is hardy with me, but I don't tempt Providence and take cuttings every autumn.

Polygonums have a bad reputation because some of them are too rampageous for words, but the late-flowering *P. affine** is quite restrained, and when it starts its succession of pink spikes it doesn't stop, nor does *P. vaccinifolium*,* which does the same thing in a smaller way. I am fond of bright candy pink, and so I like *P. bistorta*,* which has pink roots, pink shoots and fluffy heads of pink until late in the year.

*Chelone barbata** now calls itself a penstemon. It is not like the ordinary herbaceous penstemons as it makes a flat mat of foliage and throws up endless spikes of coral-pink tubular bells. It is a plant that I think needs a little support as the spikes are very long and not very sturdy. *Chelone obliqua,* on the other hand, is quite a sturdy, bushy plant, with large flowers of lilac pink for weeks in late summer.

I think everyone must know by now what I think of *Geranium endressii,* so I won't say any more about it except that it blooms on and on like an angel. The common form of *G. sanguinaria** does it, too, and though the colour is crude, there are places where I am glad to have it and where its wandering ways can't do any harm.

Scabious is an amenable plant so long as you don't divide it until the spring. I think most people still prefer the old favourite 'Clive Greaves'*, with its soft mauve flowers. There are half a dozen other blues, and a delightful white, 'Miss Willmott'*, and they all flower well. I don't say you get a lot of flowers out of season, but I do find stray blooms all the time up to Christmas.

If anyone asked me what plant has the longest flowering season of all I would say, without hesitation, a China Rose—*Rosa chinensis**, if you want to look it up. We were lucky because we found one blooming beside the garden door when we bought our house. It is still there, and it is still blooming. Although I am writing this in the middle of January there are over a dozen pink roses on the tree, and this on a north wall. I have just put in two more China roses, a Blush China and *R. chinensis mutabilis**, a brick red. My green rose is a member of the same family, and it, too, blooms out of season, but I don't think many people beside myself would say it adds much to the gaiety of the garden.

Shrub potentillas don't bloom in the winter; in fact, they don't look at all nice in the cold weather, and have that shrivelled appearance that makes you wonder if they will recover in the spring. They do, of course, quite early in the year, and then they flower non-stop till late November. So I think they are good in an all-the-year garden, but not in a position where their bedraggled appearance catches the eye in the winter. For all-round cheerfulness *P. farreri** is good value. The foliage is a bright grass green and the flowers quite a bright yellow. In my own garden I don't want more than one *P. farreri**, but I don't mind how many little bushes of *P. vilmoriniana** I have, with grey-green leaves and cream flowers. *P. purdomi* is a charmer, too, with primrose-coloured flowers, and it is a good late flowerer to boot.

Tree mallows will go on flowering until the winter. There are two at least with pink flowers, and a blue trailer called 'Primley Blue'. These shrubs get rather big, and their stems are not really stout enough to take a buffeting. A high wind knocks them about, but they are easily trimmed and I always cut mine down to ground level in spring. Some friends of mine in Dorset grow a pink mallow beside *Buddleja* 'Royal Red' in their front garden. When the two shrubs are out together, the effect is surprisingly good, and when the buddleia finishes flowering the mallow continues until the winter.

Some of the veronicas bloom early and late. It takes a year or two before the fine-leaved *V. salicifolia** starts to flower, and then it is quite a big shrub. But once started it goes on, and I often find its long white flower sprays in winter. My little friend *V.* 'Morning Glory'* does it, too, and often has more flowers in the winter than at any other time. *V. catarractae** is quite small, but a busy little shrub for all that, with little white or mauve flowers all the time. The flowers are lovely when you take the trouble to look into them; the white ones have red centres.

For endless colour in the second part of the year, I recommend hydrangeas, the ordinary *hortensis* type. When they start, they go on, and are still attractive when their flower-heads turn maroon and green and crimson and assume a papery texture. I don't even dislike them when they are quite brown; in fact, I don't cut their flowerheads off till the spring, as I like them better than bare stems.

When I decided to plant hydrangeas in my front garden, I was criticized by superior gardeners because I hadn't included any species, but had concentrated on the ordinary ones in their varying shades of pink and cerise. Since then, I have taken that advice and have a few aristocrats, *villosa**, *paniculata* and *mariesii**. They are lovely and have quality, and I am glad to have them, but their season is short and when they have finished flowering I want to forget about them till next year.

~ 10 ~

Hardy Cyclamen

I have never kept a note about the dates when my cyclamen come into flower, but I believe if I did, I should find that there was hardly a day in the year when one or other of these hardy little plants did not show a bloom or two. The spring ones overlap with those that bloom through the winter; then another lot come and go on all through the summer, when we have the great autumn display which continues until we catch up with the winter lot again. I find hardy cyclamen most fascinating in every stage of their development, and there is always something to study. If one had a cool greenhouse and could include all the near-hardy ones as well, there would never be any trouble in finding something to do. I do have one pan of *C. persicum* in a window of my malthouse, which stays there all the year. hard and dry in summer, and regularly watered in autumn when the leaves begin to show and all through the winter when there are lovely flowers on graceful stems. But it is the tiny hardy cyclamen that I really love, so small and dainty and yet so sturdy.

For some reason, they are still not grown as universally as one would expect, and I think it may be that people are so used to the winter-flowering house cyclamen, which is anything but hardy, that they cannot believe that the smaller, daintier branch of the family can possibly be the tougher strain.

It isn't often that I am generous enough to give away cyclamen corms, because cyclamen are one of the plants of which one never has enough. But I have occasionally got the better of my meanness in this respect, and I have always found it difficult to convince the recipient that this cyclamen really is hardy. 'Mustn't I give it a little shelter in the winter?' or 'Wouldn't it like to be put in the greenhouse during the frost?', 'What about a handlight?' are frequent questions, and whatever I say, I feel certain that the poor little plant is going to be treated as a lap-dog and pampered to death. As a lecturer once said—more plants are killed by kindness than by neglect.

So if you go in for the more usual outdoor cyclamen, you can be assured that they are hardy. The less hardy ones are *persicum* and *africanum* and those from Cyprus, Greece and the Lebanon, all of which are used to being baked in the summer and do not understand the meaning of our cold winter rain, so that they seldom flower out of doors. But they are the rare and expensive varieties, and are not listed in many catalogues.

There are several reasons why cyclamen appeal to me so strongly. They are among the prettiest and daintiest flowers one can have, they come at times when there are not many flowers about, and they don't mind a bit where they grow. Once you have planted them you can forget about them; they will come up regularly each year and seldom give any trouble. The first time I really noticed them was in an old garden which had an avenue of tall yews. Under each yew there was a small square bed, and each bed was as full as it could be of white neapolitan cyclamen. It was a wonderful sight to see those dancing, fluttering little flowers, like a bed of hovering white butterflies, and it decided me I must grow cyclamen.

Neapolitanum* are the ones most usually grown, and the pink are more common than the white. I am told by experts that whereas the pink forms always have pink children, you cannot rely on the progeny of the albino being white. I have not proved this, but a nurseryman friend gave me startling figures of the number of pink babies that came from a batch of white seed.

Sometimes our neapolitanum* friends are called hederaefolium* because their marbled leaves are slightly reminiscent of ivy. They bloom in the autumn and the flowers appear before the leaves. One day you have a bare patch of ground, and the next—or so it seems—it is covered with the buds of this ravishing flower. Soon the buds have turned to flowers, and there are cyclamen in all shades of pink and white, to delight the eye for many a day. When the flowers are beginning to slow down and nearly all the buds have opened, the leaves appear. They are nearly all different in their shape and marbling, but all are attractive, and I think cyclamen could well be grown for the beauty of the leaves alone.

The winter-flowering species are the ones that really endear themselves to me, as they come when they are least expected, and they stay in bloom for a very long time. The buds appear very early, and you see them lying on top of the soil, rather like a baby with its head on a pillow. You begin to get excited and watch them day by day, but they stay like this for several weeks and you begin to wonder if they are ever going to open. And then at last one day you are rewarded by an open flower and you know that you will be enjoying winter cyclamen for many weeks.

Now all the round-leaved, winter-flowering species seem to be lumped together in one category, orbiculatum*, after the shape of the leaves. I notice nurserymen continue to name them as they always have, and so I shall give the names of mine under which I bought them and know them. C. ibericum*, for instance, was the name under which I bought the one that flowers first with me, in red, pink and white, and all kinds of delightful in-between shades. Verna*, atkinsii* and hiemale* follow very soon. They all look very much alike, and I have never discovered wherein lies the difference—if any. They all have small, dark, round leaves, very slightly marbled and lined with red. There may be a slight botanical difference invisible to the layman, and it may be that the new group name of *orbiculatum** has been introduced because they are so difficult to distinguish. I think *pseudibericum* still keeps its name, although the notched leaves are more round than *neapolitanum**, for instance. They are almost heart-shaped and the flowers are pink. I have been trying to get *pseudibericum* for many years. The first I bought under that name has smooth round leaves and little pink flowers, like *atkinsii** or *ibericum**. Now I possess the real one, and there is no mistaking it.

C. coum is my favourite of all the winter ones. To be correct, I know I should call it *C. orbiculatum coum,* and if it makes it feel any better I will. It is the last of the winter-flowering ones to come out, and it is worth waiting for. *Coum* to me is the deepest cerise, but many experts think the pink variety is the one to get top marks. It is certainly bigger in every way than the cerise, but the colour is not so clear or lively. To see *C. coum* (my cerise one) in full flower on a winter's morning is something you'll never forget. It positively twinkles and sparkles in the wintry sunshine, especially if grown in grass that is heavily spangled with melting frost. There is a white variety, too, which has a crimson blotch. *Coum* leaves are the darkest and roundest of all, and are lined with crimson. They have no markings at all, and to me—an amateur at the game—they are the only winter ones I can be completely sure about. But they are all lovely, and you cannot but admire their courage and endurance. Frost, snow or wintry rain affect them not at all. They take no notice of the weather, and flower just as though it were midsummer.

Repandum is the next to appear. Its leaves, which are marbled and deeply serrated, come first; then in March and April the flowers come along. They are rather larger and longer than the other species, and are shaded from pale pink to deep carmine. Most cyclamen flowers are blotched rather than shaded, but in *C. repandum* the paler colour merges into the deeper. Once established, you'll never lose *repandum.* It seeds itself very readily and flowers faithfully every year, bringing a few more friends with it each season.

Cilicium and *europaeum** come in the summer. *Cilicium* is the smallest, daintiest one of them all, with thin, slightly twisted pale pink petals. *Europaeum** is pink and scented. It is worth going down on one's creaking knees and putting one's head under a cypress to get the exquisite perfume of this little flower. Unfortunately, *C. europaeum** does not flower as generously for me as the others do, nor have I ever found a seedling of it, but there are odd blooms all through the summer and the leaves remain above ground nearly all the time, and I am told that is a sign that it is happy.

Hardy cyclamen don't mind where they grow, and they are particularly happy under trees. I have seen them colonized under oaks and ilexes. They settle down happily under chestnuts, and they revel in the shadow of a hedge.

I first started my cyclamen under the little cypresses which border the path through the terrace garden. Now that I have many descendants of those first pioneers, I am trying to get them under all the little hedges of *Lonicera nitida* which break up the garden. But one thing is important when growing them under hedges or close to trees that have to be clipped, and that is to protect them when the clipping has to be done. Cyclamen like to be planted very near the surface of the soil, and they'll work themselves up there if planted too deep. We cut our little cypresses in August just when the first buds of *Cyclamen neapolitanum** are coming through. A lot of those little buds were broken off, and even some of the corms were gathered up with the clippings before I realized what was happening. Now I have squares of hessian to go under my little cypress trees when they are getting a hair cut, and a long strip of hessian goes under the hedge. In this way, the cyclamen are safe.

Some cyclamen seed themselves very generously. I used to think that the coiled stem with the seed-pod at the end was cunningly designed by nature to act as a spring to fling the seeds far and wide, but I don't think that this is so, because on investigation you will see that most of the seeds come to life right on top of mother, particularly if she is a very large lady. Some will be nearby and a few do appear some distance from the parent plant, but this may be due to mice, who love cyclamen seeds. When the flowers begin to fade, the flowerstems coil themselves up to bury the seed-pods in the earth, and disappear under the forest of leaves. One thinks no more about them until the following summer when the flowers are due to appear, and then, if one is lucky, there will be found fat little pods of nearly ripe seed. I remove the pods, and sow these sticky seeds when ripe because I don't want the mice to have them. If left to themselves, and mother is young and slender, there will be a little colony of seedlings right beside her. But this is impossible when the parent is four or five inches across.

I often wonder what happens to all those tiny seedlings which come to life on the old lady's chest if they are not removed. Believe me, it is the most uncomfortable place I know for any baby to grow up, and I doubt if many of them do if left there. Mine never arc. With a blunt knife I extricate those tiny corms, each with a threadlike stem and a tiny leaf, from the intricate jungle on mother's bosom. It needs a lot of care and patience, and I feel I am being awfully familiar with mother, poking my knife about among her defences, but it is surely kinder to preserve the young lives and give them a comfortable home in which to grow into sturdy youngsters.

Pink *neapolitanum** cyclamen give me the biggest haul. I find a few on the white, and I have several corms of *ibericum* and *atkinsii* which let me remove a certain number of infants from their persons, but I have never managed to get any seeds from *C. coum* or *europaeum**. I should like to know the reason for this curious form of child-raising. Is it a kind of selective breeding to ensure the survival of only the strongest progeny?

There is another way of increasing cyclamen, but it takes a lot of nerve to adopt. I believe that some growers cut up their corms like slicing a cake, making sure that there is a tiny shoot on each slice taken. I have cut very large white *flea politanum* corms into four when I wanted to get enough parents to fill the space under one particular hedge. They haven't minded a bit, and got on with their job of blooming as if nothing had happened. They can be divided the other way, too. Some years ago, I wanted to move a corm which was far larger than I had anticipated. It was tightly wedged among the roots of a willow, and in getting it up I broke it horizontally, leaving the lower stratum in the ground. I left it there and covered it tenderly with earth, feeling very much ashamed of myself. The top piece was duly and hopefully planted elsewhere, and I thought I was the poorer by one very large cyclamen. But not a bit of it. Next autumn there was a little forest of flowers and leaves on each piece of my poor mutilated friend.

~ 11 ~
Ground-Cover

Among other things there are two things I fuss about in the garden. I don't like weeds and I don't like to see great expanses of bare earth. I never see a weed without wanting to get rid of it then and there—and there is usually something else I am supposed to be doing then and there. And as for bare earth—well, it has the same effect on me. I feel I must always be harassing it, to get rid of the weeds and to prevent the surface becoming dry and caked. In spite of all the nice things I give it, my clay soil always manages to come up on top, and I spend my life trying to cover it up and in the covering-up process conserve the moisture.

Another reason why I use a lot of ground-cover plants is to make a good background for my flowers. I like to grow interesting and colourful plants, but I don't want mine to be a garden of specimens but a cohesive design that is pleasant even when the major attractions are not in flower. I have seen too many gardens in which some things are very beautiful and the rest neglected in a bare or untidy way.

My idea of a good ground-cover plant is one that has good foliage all the year round, doesn't take too much nourishment from the soil, and is easy to control. Of necessity, it must have a slightly invasive disposition, but should restrict its wanderings to the surface of the soil and not go burrowing feet down. I don't think it is necessary to be too superior about covering your ground, and sometimes the most ordinary plants are the most effective. I have seen the ordinary wild woodruff looking lovely in the shady part of a cultivated garden. It gets bigger and more luxuriant in cultivation. I have a lot of the cultivated woodruff, *Phuopsis stylosa,* which has small tufts of pink flowers at the end of every long trail. It does not insist on sun or shade, and covers a lot of ground. I like the way it goes on blooming from early summer until October and November, and the light green of its feathery foliage is a pleasant foil for many plants. London Pride (*Saxifraga umbrosa*) is another good commoner, and will do just as well in poor soils.

When I first started gardening, I used the ordinary bugle in my flower-beds. It did the job very well, but had no idea when to stop. I have never met such an exuberant plant; it over-bugled everything, and I still find it trying to get another foothold in beds where I once grew it and from which it was banished—officially—many years ago. I still use it on banks and in odd corners, because I know no better foliage, so bright and shining and bursting with good health, and the sturdy spikes of blue are exceedingly pleasant. It always looks at home and when I find it trespassing, it goes to my heart to have to fork it out, and I am always glad when I can find a good home for the poor, unsuspecting creature. I have a form with white flowers, but it is not very robust and I am having a hard time to get it to increase like its buxom sister.

There are refined forms of bugle which can be relied on not to overplay their hand. *Ajuga pyramidalis* (syn. *genivensis)* is a delightful plant, with slightly hairy and burnished leaves, and neat spikes of the most intense blue. Unlike the other bugles, it increases in itself instead of flinging out skinny arms far and wide, each finished with a tuft of a plant and ready to pin itself down in any available spot. The variegated bugle does this, but it is much less robust than the ordinary form and does its encroaching in rather a cringing, meek way. Red-leaved bugle *(Ajuga reptans rubra*)* is a wonderful carpeter for silver plants. It will grow so thick that no weed could possibly find a space in which to grow. The three-toned variegated bugle always reminds me of a tortoiseshell cat. Its correct name is *Ajuga reptans multicolorus*,* and that is what it is, with a metallic sheen to its bronze background. It makes a good background to either gold or silver plants, and associates well with plants with glaucous foliage.

I have one gardening rule—when in doubt plant *Geranium endressii.* I have never known such an accommodating plant. It never seems out of place. Put it among the aristocrats and it is as dignified as they are; let it romp in a cottage garden and it becomes a simple maid in a print dress. There are flowers all through the summer, and they don't disagree with anyone. It creeps a little and so makes a fine ground-cover plant, but it doesn't prance over everybody like the bugle. I like the places in which it seeds itself, holes in the paving or crevices in a wall. It seems to know the bare patches that I want to cover with kindly vegetation. I am quite happy with the ordinary form, but the concensus of opinion is in favour of the improved 'Wargrave'* variety, with flowers a little warmer pink. Then there is *G. endressii* 'A. T. Johnson'*, with silver-pink flowers on fifteen-inch stems. It is pretty in a border, but is more tufted than my common plant and not so useful for ground-cover.

The prunellas make a nice thick carpet of dark green. The flower spikes are not very tall and they are usually about the same height so that in early summer we change from a green carpet to a rose or blue one. The pale blue 'Loveliness' is well named and has flower-spikes a little taller than the pink and red. The rich purple *P. grandiflora* is taller still. I have only one complaint against the prunellas and that is the way they scatter their young. I wouldn't mind so much if I knew to which family I should return the little dears, but there is no way of telling until they flower, except with *P. webbiana*,* which has jagged leaves instead of the smooth ones of the rest of the family. Prunellas do well in shade as well as sun, but they need a thorough grooming after flowering and look unsightly until the untidy flower-heads are cut off and we get back to our green carpet.

Another family closely allied to the prunellas used to be called betonica, and now the awkward people who change names have decreed that it must in future be stachys. The only member of the green-leaved family that I use for ground-cover is the violet S. grandiflora*. It has handsome hairy foliage and flower-spikes about nine inches high. The pink form I find less robust, with slender flowers and slender leaves, and the white version is even more restrained; in fact, I have no luck at all with her, whatever I do she remains a mean, wizened little thing with no appetite for life. The silver-leaved Stachys lanata* is one of my favourite plants. It is a wonderful carpeter, and looks particularly well associated with bronze foliage such as Lobelia cardinalis and purple rhus. When used as a carpet, I usually cut off the tall flower spikes but I give them their head when I grow it in paving or in a wall. It is quite effective under bush roses.

And this leads me to another branch of the labiataes—the lamiums. Yes, dead nettles can be quite decorative if used in the right way. The most plebeian, of course, is Lamium maculatum, which I find rather a trial as it seeds itself everywhere and is another of those complacent intruders I find it difficult to expel because it is really an attractive plant, whether we have just the striped grey-green leaves or when covered with orchid-pink flowers. I know one garden where it is used most effectively to cover bare earth under a hedge, and I know of nothing better for banks and stone work. I don't admit it to the more select domain of my terraced garden, but I would welcome the lovely pink form and the white. There is an interesting golden version of L. maculatum, which I would use all over the place if I had enough of it. I was given a small piece years ago; it did well for me and everyone wanted a bit. I used to meet it in the gardens of friends of friends, so it was distributed very widely. But I very nearly lost my own plant because of the depredations, and spent several anxious months nursing back to health the fragment I had left myself. I have discovered that it roots very easily in a cold frame in pure sand, and when good roots have formed, it seems happiest in damp, heavy clay. I used to try peat to pep it up, but it didn't do the trick. One day, I hope to have enough to make that glinting sheet of gold I'd like to see running up between some of my more sombre plants or for a gold and silver border. There is a larger, coarser lamium, L. ovata*, which is useful when something bold in the way of groundcover is wanted. In April, it gets quite gay with cherry-red flowers.

One of the best ground-cover plants I know for a shady situation is L. galeobdolon luteum variegatum*; in other words, a variegated dead nettle with yellow flowers. But that doesn't really describe this most attractive plant. The leaves are large and are mostly shining silver against a grey background, and the flowers are deep primrose. But it isn't a plant for a small part of a neat little bed. It likes to hurl itself down a shady bank, pegging itself down as it goes. I was so pleased with the first scrap I acquired that I gave it a place of honour at the top of the peat garden, but it didn't stay there long. Very soon, it had covered one end of the garden, and was walking across the bottom of the ditch to get busy on the other side. Most of it had to be removed, and now it glints under silver birch trees. I often see unsightly shady spots in gardens, and think how nice they'd look if clothed with this symphony in green and silver. Used on a hillside, it would almost give the impression of a waterfall.

We grow *Aster yunnanensis* 'Napsbury'* for the lovely mauve and orange daisies in the summer, but it also makes a good thick carpet, and by the time autumn comes, the ranks will be closed and there will be a close planting of shining leaves.

Symphytum grandiflorum* is pleasantest in the spring when the cream, apricot-tinged flowers hang above large hairy leaves. There isn't much competition when it is in flower, and I can get quite a thrill seeing it thrusting through the railings of a forgotten garden or blooming away madly in a quiet corner of my own. I forget then that it grows coarse and dull in the summer, and I usually plant it in those places which become a tropical jungle in high summer, and so I don't see much of it after its glory is over.

Periwinkles lost their Victorian popularity early this century, perhaps because they were tangled up in our minds with rockeries and grottoes and other Victorian horrors. Now they have come into their own again with a vengeance, not so much in flower-beds, where they'd be rather too busy, but to cover the ground among shrubs. Large nurseries who design labour-saving gardens of shrubs and trees use vincas by the thousand.

I have always had a few periwinkles in the garden and would hate to be without them. The large blue flowers of *V. major* have an innocence and purity hard to find in any flower. It put itself in the wall that shields me from the road and I am delighted to have it there, but I do curse it somewhat when it pops out of the wall for richer living in the border, although its wide-eyed flowers in winter soften me. In the right place, it is an invaluable ground-coverer; there is nothing better for thickening up the bottom of a mangy hedge or providing a welcome green flurry at the bottom of a wall. I have seen it curbed to a narrow band at the edge of a path, and holding up a bank with loops and trails of shining green. The variegated form is nearly as lusty and often more effective. There is one form called *elegantissima** which looks as if white paint had been brushed on dark green and I don't wonder the flower arrangers use the long trails, each with its lovely floral ending, in winter bowls. The other, *V. major reticulata*, is variegated with gold.

The upright *V. difformis* is also in the large-leaved section, and has pale, pale flowers in winter. I have been told that it is not always hardy in cold parts of the country, but it grows happily in Somerset. *V. difformis* is smaller in leaf than *V. major* and a little larger than *V. minor*, with curious shaped, rather spidery flowers in lavender blue.

The biggest group of periwinkles are the small-leaved ones, *Vinca minor*. Records show that there have been at least fifteen different forms, but, alas, I don't know if they all exist today. Has anyone the double form of *V. minor alba*, or *V. minor roseoplena**, a double red, or *V. minor cuprec*, which is a single in reddish-copper? I know two different white ones, the ordinary *V. minor alba* and Mr Bowles's variety, with different-shaped flowers, and two single blues, the ordinary one and the more intense 'La Graveana'*. There is a pink, a burgundy-coloured, and one that goes as *V. minor rubra plena*, which has a few extra petals but is not really double. *V. m. caeruleo-plena**, sometimes called 'Celestial'*, is really double, with flowers like little blue roses. The ordinary variegated form has silver markings and blue flowers; *alba variegata** has gold markings and white flowers; there is a blue-flowered form with gold variegations and a gold-leaved vinca which can have white or lavender flowers.

I use violets to cover ground in shady places, and can also recommend alpine strawberries as carpeters of the most determined calibre. They work fast and give dividends, if one has time to collect. I have just started growing the 'One-leaved Strawberry' and the fascinating little 'Plymouth Strawberry' with its green flowers, and there are other members of the strawberry family that provide attractive foliage and pretty little white flowers, but I think if one is growing wild strawberries, one might as well have the fruit as well. I have the white 'Pine Strawberry' and 'Baron Solemacher', both of which are of the bushy type and better as an edging than a carpet.

Tiarella cordifolia loves a shady, rather moist position and then it creeps about at a prodigious rate, its flat, well-marked leaves making a lovely background for the cream 'foam' flowers in spring. Mitellas have the same habit, with smaller, darker foliage, and white flowers. *M. diphylla* is the most attractive. *Asarum canadense* has large, heart-shaped leaves in dark and shining green and does well in shade, too.

In American gardens, one sees sheets of pachysandra under the trees and shrubs, and it is quite effective and certainly no weed could penetrate such close vegetation. The variegated form is more exciting but takes much longer to get going. 'English ivy' is much treasured in the States, and is used in the same way as pachysandra. But I don't think it is quite such a tough plant, for although I have never heard wails of grief over lost pachysandra, there are bad winters when all the precious ivy is caught. We regard ivy as more of a nuisance than a help, although I have seen most effective use made of it in churchyards and parks, where it is trained to make even bands of close dark foliage. It needs very regular and drastic trimming, but is tough enough to stand up to it. There is a vogue at the moment for interesting little ivies, some variegated, others with particularly well-cut leaves, and these used as groundcover make pleasant designs between shrubs or among woodland plants.

Feathery foliage is pleasant as a background for very severe, swordlike plants. Fumitory (*Corydalis cheilanthifolia*) is soft and a very pleasant shade of green, and the bronze form is particularly attractive. For years, I have planted the double spiraea in odd spots that need clothing. It used to be called *Spiraea filipendula flore pleno**, but now with its rise in importance, the spiraea has been dropped and it has become *Filipendula hexapetala**. It has curious hanging roots like miniature elongated dahlia tubers, with a fibrous root system as well, and hugs the ground with dense, ferny foliage. The double cream flowers come on red stems about two feet high, and the flowerbuds are pleasantly tinged with pink.

In some cases, bedding plants can almost be classed as groundcover. Every year I buy boxes of annual lobelia in white, pale blue and deep blue, and plant them between my taller plants. Very soon, they become thick carpets of colour winding away into the forest of perennials, and I keep my pleasant carpet of colour until frost occurs and their little day is over. *Ageratum* can be used in the same way and makes a solid carpet.

There are some dwarf perennial plants that can be used in the same way. *Bellis perennis,* with shaggy flowers in white or pink, blooms on and off till Christmas, and whenever there is a blank space near the front of the border, I stud the ground with divisions of *Bellis* 'Rob Roy', and the exquisite little 'Dresden China' daisy and its white counterpart 'The Pearl'. The double Sweet William—*Dianthus barbatus flore pleno*—which cottagers call King Willie, isn't really a perennial, although an occasional plant will survive several seasons. It is worth keeping a supply of cuttings going for that carpet of deep velvety crimson which is so effective if all goes well, but the plants do straggle occasionally and sometimes have a tendency to rot, so that although I love it dearly, I wouldn't pin all my faith on it.

Certain shrubs, too, have excellent ground-cover properties, such as *Cotonester horizontalis,* both plain and variegated, and the dark-leaved spreading *Viburnum davidi. Cytisus kewensis** is a great feature of my garden in early May, when its sheet of cream loveliness drips over the wall, but it is a great ground-cover plant, too, and there are no weeds in the square yardage it covers. Hypericums have long been used for covering large areas with dense vegetation, particularly *H. calycinum,* an excellent and worthy plant, but like many excellent and worthy people rather dull. I think I like better the horizontal honeysuckle, *Lonicera pileata,* which has only to be introduced to a bare patch or an ugly tree stump, and it sets to work to provide a dense and completely flat coverage of small shining leaves, frothed with small white flowers in spring, which turn in time to translucent blue berries.

Cornus canadensis is a wonderful ground-cover shrub for those lucky ones who have no lime in their soil. It is such a lovely plant that it should be used in a very special place, where the attractive foliage on three-inch stems can be admired all through the year. When each flat rosette of leaves is finished on top with a typical dogwood flower, the effect is really enchanting.

So many of the good-foliage plants are excellent ground-cover plants, too, that it is difficult to know in which category to put them. Bergenias, tellima, many of the heucheras, and perennial candytuft are useful in both ways, and I include them, too, in the list of plants I use to give the garden a clothed look in the winter. Many of the prostrate cypresses and junipers come into all three categories, too, and one can ring the changes on golds and greys, glaucous and variegated. They are permanence personified in whatever role we choose to use them.

~ 12 ~

Foliage Plants

I suppose it is mainly lack of labour that is responsible for our changed gardening ideas, but I am not sure. Even if we could afford to have all those complicated herbaceous borders that were a solid bank of colour all through the summer, I doubt if we would want them. Colour, as such, has lost the appeal it had, and I think nowadays most of us think more about an all-the-year-round garden effect. We want our gardens to be interesting and attractive rather than a riot of colour, and we have come to appreciate beauty in less obvious forms. We don't hear so much about that 'good show of colour' which used to be the highest praise in the good old herbaceous days. Today we look for beauty of form, of colour, grouping and texture, and foliage has a lot to do with it. Gertrude Jekyll, of course, knew this years ago, and she appreciated then what we are realizing today. Her books are full of ideas and suggestions that adapt themselves marvellously to our present style of gardening, and I often wonder how many of her contemporaries realized the inspiration of her teaching and carried out her ideas in their gardens.

Herbaceous borders, as such, are quite out of fashion, and it is only in very rare cases, such as a public garden or a garden school, that one ever sees a real herbaceous border, that mushroom growth that attained mountains of colour in high summer and was reduced to bare earth and a little stubble for half the year. I do not wonder that we do not attempt them now, because I think a really perfect herbaceous border is as difficult to achieve as a perfect dinner of many courses. I have always felt very humble before the cook who can produce an elaborate dinner of many courses without any of them spoiling by waiting. I know I have the greatest difficulty in thinking up two courses that will be just as good if my guests appear an hour late, and to do this with five or six courses is nothing less than a masterpiece.

An herbaceous border is just as difficult. There must always be something coming on to fill up. the gaps left by plants as they finish, and it must be so arranged that interest and colour are continual and evenly distributed. A good herbaceous border can be superb, but a bad one can be dreadful. And how is one to guard against failures and vagaries of climate, when things come out at the wrong time and the dahlia we were certain was a warm crimson turns out a shrieking orange?

My borders are all mixed, irises and bulbs, roses and shrubs; with plants of every description. My aim is to have them looking comfortable and furnished at every time of year, and this I know I could not achieve without a fair proportion of plants that are grown purely for their foliage. Bulbs are only seen for short intervals, many shrubs are deciduous and many plants herbaceous, and without my permanent plantings of foliage, the garden could be as bare as a herbaceous border in winter. Of course, many of my foliage plants do have flowers, but they are a secondary consideration, an extra dividend. It is leaves I am after, leaves in every colour and of every texture. I am not going to deal with silver plants here (they have a chapter to themselves), and though I think silver is more helpful than any other colour, silver alone won't do. We need the depth of dark green, the warmth of gold, the relief of purples and reds, and the light of variegation.

We can't depend too much on our silver, even without the threat of monotony, because so many of them are not completely dependable. A few are definitely tender, and bitter, biting winds can play havoc with some of the softer grey plants, so I feel it is essential to use a certain number of hardy evergreen plants as well.

If I were asked to choose only one such plant, I think it would be an euphorbia, *Euphorbia wulfenii**. There are several large euphorbias which look very much the same. To botanists, they are either *E. wulfenji, E. characias* (and there are two of them) or *E. sibthorpii**, but to you and me and most of the nurserymen they are all *E. wulfenii*. So I shall call my euphorbia *wulfenii** and then everyone will know what I mean.

No weather seems to daunt this handsome plant. Those lovely grey-green spikes remain calm and untouched by the bitterest weather, and if it flowers, it will do so in the winter, when its flowers will be even more welcome than in the summer.

Flowers may come and flowers may go, but that handsome mass of glaucous foliage will be there as a foil and a furnishing and a refreshment for many years. I put three plants in my paved terrace many years ago. There has been only one handsome plant for some years now, and I imagine the others were overlaid. I put in three because I wanted a solid lump of foliage right away. Now the remaining specimen is so big and spreading that I am wondering if I shan't have to start all over again some day soon. But I hold my hand while new growth comes each year from the base, but when I see the solid mass of short ends where I have cut back the finished stalks, I wonder how long it can go on.

I have never discovered how this euphorbia quite works. Would each of those handsome leaf spikes flower in time if they were left on the plant? Some get so long and straggling that I have to cut them back, and I wonder if I am sacrificing flowers in doing it. One year the plant will be one mass of flower, the next there will none that I can see; yet every year I find a few precious seedlings near the plant.

I get a lot of fun watching my euphorbias in early winter to see if they are going to flower. When the leaf spikes remain rigidly erect, I know there is not a hope, but when I see the tips beginning to bend over, I know something is going to happen. Every day they bend a little more, and become so rigid that they'd break if you tried to straighten them. I can only think that this is nature's way of protecting her young in winter weather, because directly the buds begin to open, the stems straighten out to a flower truss about a foot high, spangled with black-eyed, yellow-green flowers.

Though I grow my euphorbia by itself so that I can admire it from all sides, I have seen them used very successfully with a background. They make a pleasant screen for the lower limbs of old shrub roses, and I shall never forget coming down some stone steps in a garden and meeting a euphorbia in full flower poised at the base—and a very bare and ugly base—of a solitary yew. The bright yellow green looked lovely against its sombre background.

In another garden, a big group of euphorbias furnish magnificently a corner where two high walls meet. I have seen them massed under high trees, and in a formal winter garden I admire, a huge euphorbia stands sentinel at each corner of the rectangular planting.

There are other euphorbias that I like as foliage plants. I always leave a few seedlings of *Euphorbia lathyrus* in the garden. I think the caper spurge would be esteemed as a good garden plant if it weren't so busy seeding itself everywhere. An odd plant here and there is very pleasant, lovely in its blue-green foliage and quite exciting when topped with bright green pointed bracts in which nestle the caper-like fruits. Now that it is said to discourage moles, I think we shall see it more often.

The toughest, most intense euphorbia I have is *F. Robbiae*. The new green is tender, but it soon turns to solid, shiny, dense leaves, which turn not a hair whatever the weather. The fragile green flowers are a good contrast to such a solid base and they remain nearly as long as the leaves. I understand the first scrap of *F. Robbiae* came back to England in Mrs Robb's capacious handbag, and I am very glad it did because I find it a great comfort. It doesn't make such a big and symmetrical bush as *F. wulfenii,* as it grows sideways and all ways. I like to see it planted in a corner where nothing else looks well, or under a hedge where it can potter along in its rather uneven way. I have to admit that it does spread a little and does not always keep to its allotted space, but if we refused admittance to plants of a wandering disposition, our gardens would be dull indeed.

I love glaucous foliage in all its variations, the pointed swords of iris and the smaller foliage of pinks and dianthus. The lovely blue of Jackman's rue is a good foil for many plants. I find asphodelus rather an unsatisfactory plant because the flowers do not come out together and there are always dead among the living, but the fine foliage makes another change in the glaucous theme and so is valuable. My favourite of all the glaucous plants is *Othonnopsis cheirifolia**, and I am always surprised that more people do not grow it. The leaves are flat with rounded ends, and they grow packed on top of each other like an unopened fan. The plant likes to keep close to the ground; it puts out skinny arms which anchor themselves to the soil as they go. I assist them in the process by putting sand on the soil below them and a flat stone on top of the stem. When they have rooted themselves, I cruelly sever my new plants from mother and plant them where I will. Flowers are not the main attraction of this plant, although I am always glad to see the bright golden daisies in the winter.

Another wonderful plant with blue-green leaves is *Rudbeckia maxima.* I have discovered that it likes a damp place, and to keep the leaves up to standard—that is, very big—it should not be allowed to get big. Frequent division seems to be necessary. Again, I am more interested in the leaves than the flowers, but the flower stems have an architectural beauty of their own, so smooth and straight are they with tiny leaves where they branch. They sway in the wind but need no staking, and hold their bright yellow heads so high that they do not clash with any flowers near them. The yellow is intense, but is tempered by the conspicuous pointed black centres. This is not really a plant for the mixed border. The leaves are so huge that everything else look out of proportion. To get its real effect, I feel it should be by itself. I have seen it magnificently placed rising from a stone pavement near water.

Two small and difficult plants have this lovely foliage. In *Omphalodes luciliae* the foliage is almost blue. The best plants I know are grown vertically facing north. One is in a stone wall and the other nestling in the blocks of a peat wall. In both places, the plants look happy and their lovely foliage grows in a veritable cascade. The other plant is *Ranunculus calandrinioides,* which I think should really be given a happy home in an alpine house. It is seldom really happy grown out of doors, and to enjoy it at its best, it does need some protection.

I couldn't talk about foliage plants without mentioning bergenias. I never know whether to include them in the category of foliage or groundcover. They are, of course, groundcover *par excellence,* groundcover at the rate of one leaf per foot, but they are magnificent foliage plants as well.

We used to call them *Saxifraga megasea**, or the elephant-leaved saxifrage, and felt they were rather dull plants which one put up with but did not cherish. But not now, oh no. All the nurseries clamour for them, and if you get in a garden designer to plan your garden, you may depend on it that bergenias will figure in the design.

But it isn't only because they are useful that I enjoy bergenias. The more you live with them, the more beautiful they become. There are so many shades of green in those great fluted leaves, and as the year goes on, they turn lovely shades of red and crimson.

I think bergenias look best against stone or gravel. I know some people put them in the front of a border against a lawn, which is not really the best place for them; in fact, I think they are wasted like that, and they need continual thinning to keep those handsome leaves out of the way of the mower. I like to give them all the room they want, at the edge of a stone path or among stones on a bank. There is a long, low house where I often call, with the door in the middle, and the symmetrical design is enhanced with two massive chunks of bergenia on each side of it. Sometimes you see narrow little beds in front of houses, just wide enough to stop the drive coming right up to the house. Mean little beds they often are, primly edged with mean little tiles. That is where a hunk of bergenia makes all the difference. Instead of a hard, straight line you get a generous uneven one. It doesn't matter how far the bergenias stray over the path; in fact, the farther the better because it marries the bed into the drive. Nor do bergenias mind being grown vertically. There is a house near me where they are cleverly grown in a wall. I expect they started at the top of the wall to begin with, but now they have somehow lodged their great fat stems into ledges of stone and have crept down the wall. In January and February, when sprays of bright pink flowers peep from the giant leaves, that wall is a very pleasant sight, and I always slow down as I pass it.

They are certainly too big for any but a very big rock garden, and then I think they are a pleasant change from microscopic plants and tracts of scree. And there are so many different ones you can have. To most people, bergenia is *Bergenia cordifolia* because that is the easy, common one, and for most purposes it is definitely the best. It increases quickly and is never temperamental. Some of the others are, and they definitely do not flower so freely. I have two white forms, but have never yet had a flower on either. I don't know how many different bergenias are grown today; I know one collector who has twenty different ones, I myself have over a dozen, and I have not really started to try yet.

There is an improved form of *B. cordifolia* which is attributed to Miss Jekyll. The pink flowers are finer and come on taller stems. I have a miniature form of *cordifolia* for which I have never been able to get a name. I was given the freedom of a forgotten garden to take whatever I wanted, and the only thing I discovered among the dandelions and docks was this tiny little bergenia. It has never flowered for me, but a piece I planted on someone else's wall flowered the first year, little pink flowers just a shade smaller than ordinary *cordifolia*. One of my favourite is *B. ciliata,* with the most entrancing pale pink flowers. The edges of the leaves are very hairy and always remind me of dogs' ears. Another I like is *B. purpurascens,* with very large and handsome leaves and intense carmine flowers on tall carmine stalks. It is most handsome, and I admire it, but I haven't quite the same affection for it as I have for the chubby pink flowers of *B. cordifolia,* with their glistening green stamens.

I think it takes all kinds of foliage to make a garden, the ferny leaves of *Spiraea filipendula*,* with its hanging bulbous roots and creamy white flowers, or the feathery leaves of fumitory (*Corydalis cheilanthifolia*), sometimes bronzed. The flowers of the tall *Chrysanthemum macrophyllum** are rather dull, but the leaves of the plant are beautifully cut and a good shade of green. I love the foliage of all the heucheras and tiarellas, particularly one I call *Tellima grandiflora* but which I am assured is really a heuchera. They are evergreen, and colour so well in autumn that I think no garden should be without them.

I am sure different coloured leaves help the garden picture considerably, and that is why I use as many variegateds as I can. It is not everybody who likes variegated foliage; in fact, some people dislike it intensely. My husband did, and couldn't understand why I wanted mottled and striped leaves when I could have perfectly good plain green. Walter always maintained that variegation signified disease, and if there was one thing he hated, it was anything he thought wasn't healthy. So in his lifetime I had to curb my collecting fever, and it is only of recent years that I have filled the garden with all the variegated plants I can get. Some of them, of course, don't keep their fascinating leaves in the winter. The variegated kerria doesn't, for one, but how lovely it is when the leaves unfold in early spring. It is one of the daintiest little shrubs I know, never very big and pleasantly spreading. I like variegated rue, for a change, and couldn't rest until I had run to earth variegated forms of *Iris pallida* and *foetidus**. Variegated figwort (*Scrophularia nodosa variegata*)* is a very showy plant with wide, heavily marked leaves, and the variegated horehound has smaller leaves, rather speckled, and is a much smaller plant. I saw the figwort used successfully in borders recently; a group of five or six makes a good solid patch of lightness that will remain the same all through the season, whatever flowers may come and go. I love the variegated bugle for covering ground under dark plants, with its touch of pink when there is frost. But I think my favourite of all is my precious variegated mint, *Mentha rotundifolia variegata*;* although, alas, it dies to the ground in the winter. The green is the softest, gentlest green I know, and there is more white in it than in many variegations. Some of the leaves are completely white or slightly tinged with pink, and it is these that I use among the flowers in my bits and pieces bowl.

Variegated *Veronica gentianoides* is a good-tempered plant with its neat shining leaves and neat markings of cream and rose. I am not sure how many different forms there are of the variegated *Vinca major*. I think at least three, one with deep cream variegations, another paler that looks as though it had been splashed with white paint and is, I think, the one called *elegantissima**, and another with smaller, narrower leaves. I know two variegated forms of *Vinca minor*, one is marked with silver and has blue flowers, and the other has golden variegations and white flowers. Among the smaller plants, I like to see a patch of variegated arabis tumbling between the stones, and I put my tiny variegated aubrieta in a trough to ensure its safety. There is a variegated rock rose and a variegated rock phlox, and the variegated form of *Erysimum Linifolium* is one of the most admired plants in the garden. It is not completely hardy, and I make sure I have plenty of cuttings in the frame. There is a variegated polygonum, virginia creeper, and a much treasured *Euphorbia amygdaloides*.

I wish the climbing—or creeping—*Euonymus radicans** didn't take so long to get started. There is nothing more attractive for covering a brick wall or ground under trees, but it is a slow starter. The silver variegated ivies are not much quicker, and I don't find the variegated *Daphne cneorum* at all in a hurry. I have had a small one for several years, and it hardly increases and never flowers.

Golden or bronze foliage brings sunshine to the garden. I like mounds of golden sage and patches of *Veronica teucrium trehane** with its small yellow leaves. Golden thyme and golden saxifrage give all-the-year-round colour, and so does the golden form of *Lamium rnaculatum*. The whipcord stems of *Veronica edinensis** and *loganioides** are glossy and bronzed, and so is the bigger bush *Cassinia fulvida**. There are many golden conifers both small and big, and often a good effect can be made with a golden euonymus or privet.

Downy foliage strikes another note. There are not many plants with the heavy felted leaves of phlomis, but there are several members of that family that can be used for a softening, subduing effect in the garden. The most common, of course, is *Phlomis fruticosa* with grey-green leaves and whorls of golden flowers, in *P. 'E.C. Bowles'** the flowers are paler in colour, and in *P. chrysophylla* there is a distinct yellow tinge in the leaves. *P. viscosa** is like a big herbaceous plant, with large heart-shaped leaves and hairy flowers of greenish-cream and pink. *P. italica* is different again. The leaves are smaller and whiter, and it grows in an awkward niggling way, putting out a foot here, drawing it back and trying elsewhere. I grow it against a wall where its lack of symmetry is not so noticeable. The flowers are pinky mauve and not as striking as the yellow-flowered tribe.

I have one other flannel-leaved plant that is very dear to me. At first I thought it was a dwarf phlomis, then discovered it was a form of horehound and delighted in the name of *Marrubium candidissima**. I established that name in my head, and then the higher-ups decided it wasn't a marrubium but a ballota, and now I have to refer to my notebook every time anyone asks me what it is. I can never remember *Ballota pseudodictamnus,* but I ought to because I have several plants of burning bush in the garden. The ballota makes a lovely hump of grey-green, and I have my best plant at the side of the little crooked path, so that it comes over the path on one side and over the tiny wall on the other. The flower spikes are attractive with the tiny pink flowers embedded in downy shell-like calyces close to the stem. Flower arrangers love them, but I cut them off as soon as they get the least bit untidy because I really grow the plant for its downy leaves.

Bronze and red foliage have their place, but I don't think one wants too much. I am not like some gardeners I know and buy every purple-leaved tree and shrub that grows—copper beech, purple nut, and sycamore, maples, vines, and plums and crab-apples. I have a purple rhus, *Rhus cotinus* 'Notcutt's variety'*, and grow silver-foliaged plants below it. *Berberis thunbergii atropurpurea nana** is a shrub to go in a mixed border where a pool of crimson is wanted. Purple sage is the nearest I can get to an evergreen plant with red or purple leaves. Many dahlias and lobelias have lovely red foliage, but it disappears in winter. The red-leaved bugle stays with us all the winter, and for a livelier note there is the tortoiseshell form with metallic markings in red and cream.

I think my favourite red-leaved plant is a spinach, 'Red Mountain Orach'. It is an annual and a persistent annual at that. I don't know any plant that sows itself so liberally and over so many years. I bought it once only, many many years ago, and it has been coming up intermittently ever since. I try not to let it go to seed, but it outwits me every time, and each spring I see the familiar little red seedlings appearing all over the place. It is really lovely in the right place, and in the morning sunshine or in the late afternoon when the light shines through those great red leaves, the effect is really dazzling. I like to mass it in dull places in the borders and near silver shrubs, but I cannot avoid odd plants in odd places. It has the same effect on me as kittens have. When they are very tiny, you can destroy them without too much heart-searching, but if the seedlings escape me until they are quite big, I realize how lovely they are and leave them, even though they have put themselves in the wrong places. This plant has very small roots for such a big body and wind can play havoc with it, so a little staking is necessary sometimes. I don't think I shall be popular in recommending that red spinach shall be brought into the family. I know husbands and wives who almost come to blows about it. Madame loves it for her flower arrangements and Monsieur, as the gardener, curses. I combine both roles in one person, and I wouldn't like life without red spinach!

~ 13 ~
That Patch of Silver

Although Gertrude Jekyll realized long ago the value of silver-foliage plants, I think it is only in the last few years that the vast army of ordinary gardeners have made a point of including silver subjects in their schemes.

I remember in about 1939 a local nursery appealing to me for a bit of *Stachys lanata**, and suggested that if I hadn't the plant I might be able to get a piece from one of the villagers. That now deservedly popular king of the silvers was then only a despised cottage garden plant, and did not figure in nurserymen's catalogues. If I could have only one grey plant in my garden, that would be my choice. The texture and colour of the foliage is the best of all. It is indifferent to climate or soil, and is happy wherever it happens to be planted. I have it in walls and in paving, falling over banks and great chunks of it in borders. It makes an excellent border between bed and path, and for this purpose can be trimmed to an even band and not allowed to flower. Everywhere else, its tall branching flower spikes of softest pink are a welcome feature, and I could not do without them in the house—alive in the summer—and dead in winter-time.

The next on my list used to be *Senecio cineraria.* I thought it was the most silvery of all the silvers until I met *Senecio* 'White Diamond'*, and that is so silver as to be almost white. Its leaves are not unlike the S. *cineraria,* but they are wider and more substantial, and it makes a sturdier and more compact plant. I had not realized how good it was until I met a plant I had given to the Botanic Garden in Oxford. One gets used to the plants in one's own garden, and when one meets them elsewhere, they take on a new personality. I came home and apologized to my own unappreciated plants. As well as being better to look at, it has the estimable quality of being more reliable. My poor S. *cineraria* has the regrettable habit of dying on me sometimes, always when I don't expect it, so I always take a yearly batch of cuttings. I like plants that I can rely on, and I discovered many years ago that though my friend S. *cineraria* may live happily for several winters, one particularly hard frost will turn that smiling beauty into a pathetic wreck that offends the eye; so I learned never to plant it in such a position that should this happen my whole plan would be ruined. I think I could risk 'White Diamond'* in a key position, but so far have always put her where she has a little protection to her back, such as a wall or some steps. I don't allow either of these poor things to open their flowers, as those tight little golden flowers do detract from the lavenders, pinks, and lemon shades that look so well with silver.

I find *Centaurea gymnocarpa** hardier than *Senecio cineraria,* but not so dead certain that I would dare risking a winter without a nice little collection of cuttings in the frame. I would hate to lose those long fernlike leaves that are so very graceful. Although park gardeners use it in little tufts to temper brilliant bedding effects, it really looks best grown in a mass. I always remember how Mrs Clive at Brympton d'Evercy used it in a great frothing mass against purple rhus and red dahlias in her famous red and silver scheme. If my plants are not very big, I use three or four together, with the front ones at the edge of a wall or path so that they cascade over the side. The dull mauve thistle heads are quite unworthy of such a handsome plant, and are never allowed to see the light of day.

Another good grey plant is *Senecio leuchostachys*,* and it has the added attraction of ivory-coloured flowers, which need not be removed. There is no question that it is tender, and even in Somerset does not get through the winter unless it is trained to a south wall. Another reason why I like to grow it against a wall is because it looks better this way, or poised horizontally on top of a raised bed. It is rather more feathery than the others and has not as much substance, so I like to grow it where its lack of body is not revealed.

Helichrysum angustifolium* is a good plant and effective when it gets big enough. This, of course, is the famous curry plant, and there is no mistaking it when you get near it. I hadn't realized I had it in the garden until one day I was bending over a bed and had an unmistakable whiff of curry. I 'acquire' a vast number of new plants and cuttings each year, and I must have struck this little soul and planted it out without realizing what it was. The leaves are narrow, and it grows rather like an abandoned lavender. The first flowerings are flat corymbs of dull gold at the top of each stalk, and afterwards little side shoots appear down the long stalks, each topped with a small cluster of golden flowers. This is really a very good gold and silver plant, because the gold is soft and burnished and has none of the harsh crudeness of *Senecio cineraria* and the santolinas.

I am rather frightened of giving the name of a neat bush helichrysum that is one of the joys of my life. I was given it in the beginning as *H. trilineatum*,* and I think most of the nurseries call it that, but I have been put right by a knowledgeable friend who insists it should be *H. alveolatum*,* and the name *H. trilineatum** belongs to a plant I call *Helichrysum plicatum.* I know I shall be corrected again, but I think it is safer to follow the lead of the nurseries and keep the names I know. So I continue to call my neat little bush with its narrow leaves and tiny flowers of yellow plush *H. trilineatum*.* It is a most comfortable plant, never gets too big, and there is never a hair out of place. It just sits there complacently smiling whatever the weather or the time of year.

Helichrysum plicatum is definitely more elegant, but its long, narrow silver leaves come on brittle stems and it does get rather dishevelled in the wind. And I have a suspicion that it can be affected by heavy frost. With me, it comes and goes. Sometimes I have a beautiful rounded bush, then I notice part of it is dying off, which spoils the symmetry, and next year there is very little life on its skeleton limbs, and I am faced with a gap until the next child grows up. The flowers are as elegant as the leaves and as slender. They come on foot-long stems, are in flat open corymbs, and are very small in a thin greenish gold. I cut them for drying, but take care to protect them as they are brittle.

Those are all the large silver plants apart from shrubs that are good all the year round. There are legion artemisias, but they are only good in the summer. Some keep their form in the way of bare arms and legs, but none of them can be considered good all-the-year-round silver plants. I used to think *A. Ludoviciana* was the best of the tall thin silver artemisias. It is still the whitest, but is almost too slender to be effective by itself and looks best when it is hemmed in by herbaceous plants about the same height. *A. gnaphalodes** is much more sturdy, and a good clump can look quite well without backing, so long as it is staked early and has grown up as straight as possible. *A.* 'Silver Queen'* was heralded as an even better plant, but I have two complaints. They all ramble, but 'Silver Queen'* is the worst of the lot and can't keep herself where she is put, but comes up in the middle of irises and peonies a long way off. She is bushier than the other two, but has a weak backbone and I have never succeeded in making her hold herself up, however well and early I stake. Whatever I do, she goes at the knees and flops into a feathery mass, which looks all right from the distance but is distressing close at hand.

My best artemisia is a good form of *A. absinthium,* not nearly as woody as the usual one, and making a beautiful low clump of delightful feathery foliage on stems strong enough to keep their shape. I don't know where it came from and I have never seen it elsewhere, so to distinguish it I call it *A.* 'Lambrook Silver'*. It doesn't look too attractive in the winter, but is better than the first three, which should really be cut down in the autumn. Some people leave the flower spikes on all through the winter after the foliage has disappeared; but they don't really stand up well to inclement weather, and the slender grace that charmed us in the summer looks untidy and shabby after being buffeted by winter wind and rain.

There are many other artemisias. I like the pewter-coloured *A. pontica,* that is said to look like a little cypress but quickly becomes a grove with me. *A. stelleriana* is lovely for the front of the border when its long skinny arms have their complement of white, chrysanthemum-like leaves, and as for the feathery ones, such as *splendens** and *canescens**, *discolor** and *valesiaca**, it would take someone far cleverer than I am to discriminate between them. They are all lovely and all help the garden scene. Some of them wander somewhat, but never enough to be a nuisance.

Not so fashionable as it used to be, *Lychnis coronaria,* late agrostemma, is a good silver maid-of-all-work. I wouldn't put it in a place of honour, but I do think it is worth growing in those odd places such as one finds near the back door or round the sheds, where it is pleasant to have something that looks nice and gives no trouble. It makes fine rosettes of silver leaves which cover the ground and look pleasant even when it is not in flower, and when the flowers start, they don't stop. *L. c.* 'Abbotswood Rose'* is the one best known; there is a white version which is delightful and a dainty pink one, but neither of the last two are as vigorous or as generous as the purple form.

Another plant that makes a good silver rosette, but rather smaller this time, is *Anaphalis triplinervis.* There is another very much like it called *A. nubigena**, perhaps a little taller. Both make neat tight clumps of silver and increase slowly. In the summer both produce sprays of little ivory daisies which are not unlike the popular French immortelles, and can be regarded as 'everlasting' flowers for winter drying. *A. margaritacea* is taller and has a different habit. Instead of tight clumps, it sends out feelers which show only a tiny silver rosette above ground before they grow into stalks about eighteen inches tall in a very pleasant grey-green. This plant really needs a little backing, and if one does not stake it, I think it should be grown between tall perennials. The flowers are the same ivory and very good for drying as are the two-foot *A. yedoensis**, grey-green again and with the same kind of flowers.

There is really nothing so silvery as the foliage of *Verbascum broussa**, and it is delightfully downy as well, so it is beautiful even before it sends up those tall spikes of soft yellow flowers. It does appeal to caterpillars, alas, and I find *V. haenseleri**, which is silver too, but not downy, escapes the depredations of these marauders. *Salvia argentea* is another silver-foliaged plant, even more downy than *Stachys lanata** and with a silken sheen to its down which makes it most vulnerable to winter wet, and I give it a pane of glass in the winter. Another way to grow it is vertically or under an overhanging rock, anything to keep the pitiless winter rain from beating down on its defenceless head.

Achillea clypeolata is a first-rate silver plant. It comes from Greece and has the best foliage of all the achilleas. It is almost white and cut with fernlike delicacy. Flat heads of pale yellow complete the picture, and it goes on flowering with great faithfulness throughout the summer.

A good way to get a silver effect without actually using a silver-leaved plant is to have a big clump of *Catananche caerulea major**. The flowers, of course, are blue, but the buds are silver, and give the effect of a silver cloud as they sway about in the summer air. I saw this effect in a good herbaceous border at one of the big nurseries, and I have been striving to enact it myself. Unfortunately catananche doesn't much care for my heavy clay, and I have had a hard time getting her going.

The hawkweeds are inclined to be persistent, but there is one whose persistence one can tolerate as it will introduce a silver carpet for us. All that is necessary is to plant one small rosette of *Hieracium pilosella**, and it will do the rest. Out come its little feelers, with a rosette at the end of each. Down they go and there is another little plant. The flowers are typical hawkweed, but in a pale shade of lemon that blends with everything and they come on six-inch stems. There are two other silver hawkweeds which are not at all venturesome, both make neat little plants and increase themselves by discreet seeding. *H. villosum* is, as the name implies, woolly, and *H. waldsteinii** has attractive wide leaves. Both of these hawkweeds have yellow flowers.

I have one little silver plant that came from one of the plant-hunting expeditions, and this has now been named *Chrysanthemum haradjanii**. The leaves of this plant are small and look as if they were made of light grey flannel, and each is cut to the centre along each side to give a fringed effect. It is one of those plants that everyone notices, and I grow it at the edge of a supporting wall and let it hang over the side. I can't remember if it has flowers; if it has, I have no doubt they are the usual dull yellow. It is not unlike *Chrysanthemum praeteritum**, but much more silvery and flatter in growth. I see that another of these silver chrysanthemums, *C. ptarmicaeflorum**, is now being called a pyrethrum. Two small silver teucriums for growing among stones are *T. aroanum* and *T. polium*.

It is a great pity that one can't make more use of that arch silver carpeter, *Cerastium*, but it can't be trusted. The only place where it is safe to use it is on a wall or some bare place where it can ramp to its heart's content and not swamp more worthy plants. The villagers call it 'snow-in-summer' and prize it highly, so I have to fight a losing battle with it, as I do with the village cats.

I use the silver potentilla, *P. nitida,* in paving and in my walls, and *Achillea clavenae** in the same way. The dianthus family introduce a pleasant blue-grey, and for a sink *Helichrysum marginatum** is shining silver, but it hates winter rain. Two creeping artemisias are shining silver, *A. glacialis,* which is by no means easy, and *A. lanata* (syn. pedemontana*),* which, as its name implies, walks—and it does, too, over stone or path, but not enough to be a nuisance. I have seen it used as a carpeting plant with red-foliaged dahlias and lobelias, and the combination was very good.

I wish there were more silver shrubs we could plant in our gardens. Of course, there is *Senecio greyii**, a real stand-by, which keeps its leaves and doesn't seem to mind where it grows. It flowers well, too, not such strident yellow flowers as some of the silver plants but yellow enough, and I know many people who cut them off before they come into flower. The buds are beautiful, practically white, and because they are usually mixed up with the open flowers, I don't often cut off either.

But *Senecio greyii** has, I think, one fault, and that is it grows too fast, at least it does for me. I grow it in one of my terraced beds, and I cannot let it take up too much room so I cut it back savagely every year, but there comes a time when the wood is too thick for beauty and one has to start again. Cuttings taken in July root very easily, and I think there should always be a few little plants tucked away to put in when the poor old grandmother has to go. Four or five little ones will be needed to fill the space she occupied, and as they grow, one or two can be removed at a time until only one remains, to wax stronger and stronger until she in her turn has to go.

There are three other senecios on the same lines. I believe *S. compactus** is a neater form of *S. greyii**, but I haven't managed to get hold of it. *S. laxifolius** is very similar and is, I believe, said to do better by the sea. *S. monroi** is not so silvery, although the crinkle-edged leaves have a silver lining. It makes a low, sprawling bush, good for informal work, and again is said to be a good shrub to grow by the sea.

I would not call *Phlomis fruticosa* a silver plant. The foliage is a pleasant soft grey-green, and the woolly texture makes a nice change among other plants.

I couldn't do without santolinas, and in the right place I think *S. neapolitana** is the most effective of them all. I like *S. chamaecyparissus* and its neat dwarf form, and enjoy its neat mop-heads at strategic points in the garden. I have never used it as a hedge, but have seen it used most effectively this way and I think it would be pleasant in a formal herb garden. But I think *S. neapolitana** is more graceful and feathery, and it is certainly much whiter. It looks best posed against a wall or filling up a sheltered corner. I cut off the yellow button flowers of these two santolinas most ruthlessly, but luckily I have several with sulphur flowers; but, alas, they are not quite so white and feathery as *S. neapolitana**.

I am warned that *Elaeagnus argentea** will make a big tree in time. It is taking a long time doing it. I have had it for several years and it remains about two feet tall. It has large glistening leaves like grey satin which shine as they blow in the wind. *Artemisia tridentata* is a silver aromatic bush which, I believe, grows to about three feet, although it isn't as tall as that with me yet.

Occasionally a grey-leaved tree looks well against a dark background. I have a white poplar, a whitebeam, and, at the end of the little path through the terraced garden, a kind of weeping pear, *Pyrus salicifolia argentea*,* with narrow grey leaves that flutter in the wind.

～ 14 ～
Playing with Peat

If you are one of those fortunate people with no lime in your soil, you may not realize how frustrating it is to be debarred from all the exciting things that will not tolerate lime. To begin with, one does not always realize why so many specially nice plants one buys refuse to settle down comfortably and thrive. One tries again in another position, with a few more refinements of care and soil, and very likely one goes on trying until some kind friend puts you out of your misery with, 'Of course you can't, it's a lime-hater.'

For years, I struggled with *Gentiana sino-ornata*. Everyone assured me it was the easiest of all the gentians to grow, and did not mind a little lime. I gave it pockets of pure peat or peat and sand, but dozen after dozen decided they weren't happy with me and reproachfully died. I think the reason may have been that a certain amount of lime was in the moisture that percolated to them through surrounding soil, for even those in pockets at the top of the garden wouldn't take any interest in life. It was only when I put them in stone troughs in pure peat that they condescended to try.

I had heard of the famous peat walls of Edinburgh Botanic Garden but had not then seen them, and photographs were not really much help. So my first amateurish attempts at peat gardening were not at all successful.

I chose the ditch for my operations, because I thought that it gave me just the amount of shade I wanted. The banks were given up to primroses and primulas on one side and wild strawberries on the other. I decided I could do without so many wild strawberries and would transform part of their territory into a peat garden by using blocks of peat instead of stones for the supporting walls, and filling the cavities with granulated peat.

My first mistake was not to soak the peat blocks well before I used them. Just as peat when wet holds moisture a very long time, dry peat is exceedingly dry and loses all cohesion. If I had soaked my blocks thoroughly, the plants I put in between them would have taken hold and kept them together in the drought.

It was unfortunate that we had such a dry summer that year. The granulated peat in which I had planted my subjects became as dry as dust and sifted out like sand. The small dry blocks I had used (the kind one buys for burning) became smaller and drier until they were slipping and falling like a ruined house of cards, the precious plants with them, so that in the end they just curled up and died. 'Why on earth didn't you water them?' you'll say, but I had only the lime-impregnated tap water to use, as the rain-water butts were soon exhausted, and I knew if I used that the poor things would only die another way—from poisoning instead of thirst.

Luckily, I live near the land of peat, and it was not difficult for me to get bigger, better blocks for my next venture. I explained what I wanted to my peat merchant, and he produced a load of peat 'spits'—great big pieces the same size and shape as the large pieces of stone one would use for a rock garden. This time we soaked them for days in the horse-trough in the orchard, so that they were saturated before being put into place.

The peat spits are not so hard as the solid little bits I first used, so in two or three places in the new garden we made a few stone steps to give a firm stance for walking and working in the garden.

The same cousin who remade my rock gardens made the garden for me. First he excavated all the original soil from the bank and inserted some old sheets of tin against the soil behind to keep the inevitable lime from seeping through. Then he arranged the pieces of peat in strata to give the appearance of natural outcrop, using some of the small, hard, burning blocks in such places as the top of the steps, where strength and solidity were needed, but this time we soaked them very well first. Every space and crevice was filled with granulated peat, and we took great care to ram it in well to make sure there were no air-locks when it came to planting.

Heathers were the first thing I planted. My kind cousin, who created the garden, gave it a wonderful christening present of a magnificent collection of heathers, to flower at all times of the year. Hitherto I had only been able to grow *arnea,* which does not object to lime, and though this variety comes in many colours with different flowering seasons, there are so many other lovely and exciting species which I have long envied in other people's gardens. There are a few daboecias in the collection, with their bigger bells.

All my gardening years I have been grateful that I could not grow rhododendrons and azaleas in my lime-ridden soil. Once you get the 'rhodo' (as enthusiasts lovingly call them) bug, you are finished for ordinary gardening. It seems to bite deeper and hang on harder than any other bug. 'Rhodoes', azaleas, and camellias take possession of your gardening soul. You go on buying and buying, and the deeper you go, the more expensive become your tastes. Very soon your whole garden is given up to them, and you look round with covetous eyes for more ground in which to plant rarer and richer plants. How I hope my little venture into peat gardening is not going to be my undoing! Now that I have a collection of miniature azaleas and rhododendrons snuggling among my lumps of peat, shall I have the irresistible urge to discard my faithful herbaceous plants, and transfer my affections to these fascinating subjects, transforming more and more corners of the garden into peat in which to grow more and more little 'rhodoes' and azaleas? I hope not, but I can't be certain. I have seen it happen so often before on a much larger scale.

One of my reasons for wanting a peat garden was to have a really good place for ramondas and haberleas. For some reason, they have not taken kindly to cosy little niches in my north walls, although they grow most happily for some people. There is something very fascinating about these rather aloof creatures and many colour variations, and I hope now that I have given them conditions in which they will really enjoy themselves. The peat I have used is somewhat spongy, so that it is possible to scoop a hole in it, fill it with peat mould, and plant one's treasure right in the lump of peat. I have planted my ramondas and haberleas vertically, with overhanging cover to keep off too much rain, and although the garden faces west I have found quite a number of northern aspects for them.

Cassiopes, lewisias, gaultherias and vacciniums are all good plants for peat, and the rather difficult *Calceolaria darwinii* and *C. tenella* have been given good positions. *Epigaea asiaticus** is another interesting plant I have included. I think this is what is called in America 'May-flower'. I hope so, because I am sentimental about May-flowers. When I was having an operation in a New York hospital, a cousin brought me a tight little nosegay of May-flowers to sniff. I have always preferred primroses to orchids, and though this happened over thirty years ago, I still remember how pleased I was she brought me that sweet little posy and not 'American Beauty' roses with stems a yard long.

I have not included many primulas in the garden, because I find they do just as well in any good garden soil with plenty of leaf-mould worked into it, but I have made an exception of the exquisite little *Primula clarkei* and have given her a snug little pocket all to herself, where I hope she will not be overlaid by more robust contemporaries. I have also put in *Primula forrestii,* and in the lower levels some *P. pulverulenta* 'Bartley Strain' and *P. chionantha,* to give height and variation of colour, also they won't mind if a little lime has crept into the soil, which it may well do at the lowest level.

Quite a number of nurseries and writers recommend that the petiolares primulas should be grown vertically in peat walls, under overhanging projections to protect them from rain. I have tried them this way and they have not enjoyed themselves, and I find they do very much better grown in ordinary soil with a very high proportion of leaf-mould in it. They seem to like living on a slight slope; so now I have planted them on the other side of the bank, where it is not too steep, and seen that there are projecting stones above them. These primulas have the reputation of being extremely difficult. Mine were when I tried to rear them in peat, but now that I treat them more like ordinary mortals they seem to like it better.

Shortias should revel in the peat, and I have given them a shady position, but so far they have not shown much appreciation of my efforts and have made no attempt to flower for me. But their leaves are lovely in colour, and I can at least enjoy them while I wait patiently for flowers.

Nearly all daphnes are happiest when there is a good proportion of peat in the soil. I have not wasted valuable space on the commoner varieties, such as 'Somerset'*, *pontica* and *mezereum,* but I have planted *D. collina** in a bare corner and a little *D. arbuscula* lower down. I have wedged a double-headed layering of *D. cneorum* between two big hunks of peat with a head in each direction, and have the variegated version in another place. I found *D. cneorum* very difficult until someone advised me to plant it in peat, with plenty of flat stones on top. It liked that treatment very much, and that—my fifth—attempt was successful. Masses of fragrant flowers came into bloom from under each stone, and I fondly hoped that it meant rooted layerings each time. But so far I have never had much luck in rooting the layerings, and time alone will tell if my latest venture will respond to peat treatment. *D. blagayana,* which blooms so early, I was advised, prefers a more mixed diet, so I have not planted her in pure peat. She likes a little sun, too, so she went into another part of the ditch, in a good loam, to which I added a little peat and sand to lighten it.

Cornus canadensis is an attractive lime-hating crawler, and makes wonderful ground-cover for those lucky people who can let it romp, as it works fast and covers itself with typical dogwood flowers, flat and white, gazing up to the sky. I don't imagine it will trespass too far with me. There is also a neat little knotweed (polygonum) with tiny white spikes, which does not intrude like its more dashing brothers and sisters. I have included such rarities as an orange and a double yellow celandine, the rather overpowering *Ourisia macrophylla,* with its heavy foliage and long white flower spikes in the summer, dainty little *Corydalis cava* and the intense blue *C. cashmiriana*,* and one or two small spiraeas, suitable for such a garden.

Quite by accident I have found several things that failed for me before have come into their own in peat. For years, I have been a faithful purchaser of *Saxifraga oppositifolia* from the local nursery. It looks such a healthy little plant with its chubby flower of crimsonpurple when seen in the nursery. But once in my garden, it languished and died, however carefully I chose its nook in a rock crevice. It was by chance that I discovered it liked peat, because I tried a plant in a trough in which peat was the pervading soil. Since then it has never looked back, and I have filched little bits of it to grow in the peat garden.

Phlox adsurgens is another plant about which I've made a happy discovery. Generous friends have given it to me several times. Other gardening friends have gloomily shaken heads and assured me that I'd never rear it, and up to now the Jonahs have been right. That was before I tried it in peat. My single plant has now become several, and in each case it is rambling farther afield and covering itself with myriads of healthy little shoots, each one pricking up its ears and obviously panting for adventure. *Phlox stolonifera* Blue Ridge is also susceptible to peat, and I am going to have another try at that delightful phlox, *divaricata canadensis,* which does so well in American gardens. I have attempted it several times in the past and lost it on every occasion. I am hoping that peat will work the charm.

Polygalas enjoy peat, and as they flower in the winter, I have given them good positions. The purple-flowered *P. chamaebuxus* is lovely.

Is there something in peat, I wonder, that is good for blue flowers, for it seems that a lot of my peat lovers are blue. *Meconopsis baileyi** looks happier in the peat garden than it ever has before, and of course I have included all the lime-hating gentians such as *sino-ornata* and *macaulayi*, farreri* and *hascombensis*,* and the later flowering 'Inverleith' and 'Kidbrook'* seedlings. I have blue willow gentians, and a lovely white one. Lithospermums, of course, are another tribe of blue, peat-loving flowers, and *Penstemon heterophyllus* never really lets itself go in a limy soil, but revels in a peat garden.

There are many other treasures for such a garden as mine, which I have not yet met, and no doubt I shall find so many that I shall inevitably be looking round for more bits of the garden to give over to peat.

~ 15 ~
Flowers For The House

Everyone enjoys having flowers in the house; in fact, no room really comes to life unless there are flowers or leaves or a growing plant in it, but if you happen to be garden-proud, as well as house-proud, it is very hard to keep a nice balance in the matter. It is particularly difficult in a family where one member grows the flowers and the other picks them, for nothing is more likely to disrupt home harmony.

The ideal, of course, is to have a picking border, but for those of us who haven't, I think it is only fair for the gardening side of the partnership to do the picking.

I am afraid the older I get, the meaner I am with my flowers for the house. Young beech leaves help me through the spring, climbing roses provide good material for the summer, and coloured leaves and michaelmas daisies are my stand-by for the autumn. In the winter I have my 'deads'—flowers I grow specially for drying for winter decoration.

I love my house, but I also love my garden, and my flower arrangements are never quite perfect because instinctively I choose the slightly imperfect flowers when I am picking. A crooked stalk will pass muster in a mixed bowl, and a not quite perfect bloom can be put at the back of a bowl. And when I go forth with my marauding secateurs, I snip a trifle from one clump and a suggestion from another, trying not to spoil my garden effect.

Never before has there been the intense interest in flower arrangements that there is today. Innumerable frustrated natures are no doubt satisfying the need for self-expression. Clubs, classes and competitions enable the enthusiasts to vie with each other—all excellent in their way until the devotees start playing tricks with nature. When the desire for originality results in unnatural heights and grotesque angles, the cult has gone too far. I heard at one such gathering the exponent being asked about daffodils and what could be done with them, and the answer was, 'I don't think there is anything original you can do with daffodils, you just have to put them in a suitable vase.' I ask you, who wants to be clever with daffodils?

Surely the aim in all flower arrangements should be to make them look as natural as possible; just as if they were growing, in fact. We all know that the simplest clothes are usually the most expensive; so great artistry is needed to achieve perfect simplicity.

The containers you use really decide your floral decorations, and you must have the kind of containers that go in your kind of house. I have a plain old house, with rough walls, simple heavy furniture, and stone floors. There are no mantelpieces (thank goodness) over my great stone fireplaces, and delicate pedestalled urns and vases, which are so popular for modern arrangements, are not for me. Tiny vases just look silly, and fragile glass containers are quite out of place. I use jugs of copper and mugs of pewter. My big bowls are of coarse hand-made pottery, or those lovely old wooden bread-bowls, fitted with tin linings. I find the older I get, the busier I become, and the less original in the places where I put my flowers and the containers I use. But the different seasons bring their own flowers, so there is no monotony.

Colour schemes have to be considered. In my dining-room, with its old oak pannelling, I have damask curtains of lemon yellow—sour, with a hint of green. Against the dark walls, there must be light-coloured flowers, and I ring the changes on white and ivory, primrose and yellow, and soft greens. A banksia rose is trained round the window, and when it is in bloom I have a bowl of its flowers on the low stone window-sill below the mullioned window. There is a low trough outside the window, and in it I grow a succession of flowers that harmonize pleasantly with my curtains—the perennial wallflower 'Moonlight'*, then *Gladiolus tristis grandis,* with its green-tinged ivory blooms, smelling deliciously at night. Regal lilies follow, and later I watch the capricious acidanthera to see how many of its scented flowers it will give me before frosts overtake it.

Other flowers that I find useful in the dining-room are angelica, with its great umbels of pale green, and handsome foliage, guelder roses of greenish ivory, and Solomon's seal. The green-tipped blooms of astrantia show up well against the walls, and a tall jug of the single-flowered form of *Kerria japonica* is dainty and lively. In the late autumn, there is one chrysanthemum that always finds a place in the dining-room—the fine white 'Wedding Day', with its faint scent and greenish yellow centres. Fennel is good, and foliage contrasts like rue and the variegated form of *Symphoricarpos* (the snowberry tree). *Cytisus kewensis** is excellent for small bowls, and all through the winter I have *Mahonia bealei** and winter jasmine on the table.

A large shallow bowl of lead stands on an oak table in a corner, and in it I have great fun making variations on the theme of white, green and yellow. *Iris ochroleuca** is a great stand-by for this and I wish its flowering season was longer. For just as no mixed arrangement is right without a touch of yellow, so white is the ideal companion for any shade of yellow. Orange and bronze work in with some yellows, though not all, but white is always right.

Daffodils, of course, are the happiest choice for the dining-room, and I am always sad when their season is over. As I said before, daffodils need simple treatment. I like best of all to use a shallow bowl, with a good wire or metal support, and arrange them just as though they were a growing clump, tossing their heads in orchard grass. The whole family must be there: fully-matured blooms, half-opened and unopened buds, with plenty of leaves, all put in vertically as if they were growing. To keep the illusion, a thick layer of the greenest, ferniest moss you can find should cover the support. Or they look charming in a green earthenware or pewter mug, again including buds in all stages and plenty of leaves. For the dining-room I prefer the very pale one, 'Beersheba', 'Lily Langtry' and other pale varieties.

The big hall, in which I live, has walls of greenish off-white, which are a wonderful background for any kind of flower. On a dresser on one side of the room I have a heavy glass tank, raised on an oak stand. A light tube is fixed in the stand so that the light shines up through the water and illuminates the flowers. I use every kind of flower in this tank, but I think I get more pleasure out of the first young beech leaves, and then from irises. Different types of iris, with their swordlike foliage follow one another as long as they last, and I grow as many different kinds as I can to make their season as long as possible. When most of the others are done, my old friend *ochroleuca** in white and yellow is used here as well as in the dining-room, and then come the *kaempferi** group in white and mauve and deepest violet.

On the opposite wall another dresser, longer and larger, stands between my desk and the garden door. It calls for a bigger flower arrangement, and I have a large Canton bowl that is always filled to capacity. At the height of the season I can have the most magnificent mixed arrangements, and in off-seasons a very few blooms with a background of fluttering leaves is just as effective. I can remember one of my happiest arrangements was the simplest and the most economical from the garden point of view. Against a background of young beech, I used a few pale pink Canterbury bells, with white and pale blue *Campanula persicifolia,* with a small group of the dark blue *Campanula glomerata,* and some very deep pink Canterbury bells, for emphasis.

In this room, too, there is a low stone window-sill in front of the mullion window, and on it, in the summer, I fill a sea-green bowl, originally bought for cooking, with fleshy pink loveliness, such as pale peonies, Cupid roses or hydrangeas.

But my favourite flower-piece in this room is another cooking dish that always stands at one end of the oak refectory table in the middle of the room. This is an apple-green, highly glazed, oval dish, fifteen inches long and about two inches high. It is filled with moss, saxifrage, or helxine* ('mind your own business' as it is called in this part of the world), and into it is tucked anything that happens to be available. The flowers are never the same, and it is always a great source of interest to my friends to see what I have in it. If I have only one bloom to spare, it gets full value with a background of green, and when I have plenty to choose from, I stuff it so full that no green can be seen. This happens when the walls are covered with roses, or in Michaelmas daisy time, when I can use every shade from white, through pale pink, lavender and blue to red and mulberry and violet. All through the winter, there are usually enough odd flowers to put in it, and being low one can gaze down and admire every flower that is there. It is sometimes filled with one kind of flower only, like Christmas roses or lily-of-the-valley, or there may be twenty different kinds of flowers in it. Flowers that are cut down do not give pleasure, and to be effective they should be used at their full height, but sometimes one has a single bloom of a madonna or regal lily after all the other flowers on the stalk are finished, and it can be enjoyed in this accommodating dish. I don't like to pick much of my *Daphne cneorum**, but an odd sprig or two will scent the whole house and can be snipped from the bush without spoiling it. Small plants of coloured primroses and primulas sojourn in the dish until they get tired; then they are returned to their out-of-doors quarters and fresh plants brought in. If one doesn't wish to dig up a root, it is quite easy to arrange a few flowers with leaves round them to look like a little plant, and the bowl becomes a garden.

Sometimes the dish looks like hundreds and thousands, other times there are only about six different groups. Bits of ceanothus, or japonica, leaves of *Senecio greyii, Senecio cineraria,* or *Stachys lanata** calm it down if there are too many strong colours, and in a mixed bowl like this I always try to find some very pale yellow, living flame and deep blue. You can spend as long or as short a time as you like on an arrangement like this, and be equally lavish or economical with your flowers.

I feel very strongly that flowers on a dinner-table should be low and rather unobtrusive, so as not to impede talk with one's opposite neighbour. My husband never agreed about this, and thought I was mean with my dinner-table flowers. He wanted me to use an important bowl of roses or carnations. As we couldn't agree, we compromised on a bowl of mixed fruit for winter dining and coloured ice cubes in summer. There is nothing more colourful than a bowl of fruit, and as that was in the days when dessert was a regular part of the meal, it was conveniently on the table. The ice cubes were particularly pleasant on a very hot evening. The refrigerator trays were filled with lightly tinted water—pink, green, mauve and lemon, and piled in a crystal bowl at the last minute. The hotter the night the quicker they melted, but the cooling effect was very pleasant.

Now I use a two-handled shallow pewter dish between pewter candlesticks.

106

Again I fill it with moss, saxifrage, or helxine, and poke in whatever flowers are available. I have enjoyed my meals a great deal more since I started this decoration, because I have never taken the trouble to study individual blooms so carefully before. I have discovered hitherto unnoticed wonders as I crunch my breakfast toast. Wintersweet *(Chimonanthus fragrans*),* for instance, is quite another person to me since I have had breakfast with her. The nurserymen dismiss the flowers as insignificant in their catalogues and extol them only for their heavenly scent. I don't agree. Those waxy petals, that look like miniatures of the long narrow shells one finds on the beach, are perfectly formed, and the glow of crimson which one took for granted is produced by another row of tiny petals inside the others, each one heavily veined with deep crimson. Put a mug of these flowers on a high window-sill and see them with the wintry sun glinting through them, so that they twinkle and sparkle, and you will never allow them to be called insignificant again. Christmas roses I dismissed as white with a greenish tinge until I had meals with them and made the acquaintance of an unsuspected row of tiny green nectaries inside and right at the bottom of the cup and close to the stamens.

These are only a few examples. Have you ever studied the exquisite workmanship of a scabious, for instance, with its beautiful mauve petals and a row of perfect little white rosettes round the hard green centre, that looks like an old-fashioned pin-cushion, or the green honey-tipped pistil of *Saxifraga megasea** (now known as *Bergenia megasea*),* or the individual blooms of *Mahonia bealei*,* each one of which looks like a chubby little daffodil? No one could be an atheist after studying such perfect and delicate craftsmanship.

I realize how lucky I am to live in Somerset, where flowers bloom early and late, and my coloured primroses and polyanthus start flowering in the autumn and go on till late spring. I keep the house full of them all through the winter by digging up clumps that are full of buds just about to burst, and plant them in shallow bowls, with their roots well covered with earth and the earth covered with moss. I have tried deeper bowls, but I find that in the shallow ones the plants seem happier, so long as they are kept very moist. When they begin to be less generous with their blooms, I replant them in the garden and bring in another lot.

I have one yellow polyanthus that is wonderful for this indoor culture. I found a seedling in the garden and christened it 'Lambrook Yellow'. Although it looks like an ordinary polyanthus, it has several endearing qualities. It is very sweetly scented, and the clear yellow petals, with deeper centres, are big and wavy. It is the earliest to start flowering and the last to finish—and nothing goes better with my dining-room or looks lovelier on the low stone sill.

Any coloured primrose or polyanthus can be used like this, though no other is quite so satisfactory for the purpose. *Primula* 'Wanda' planted close together can be very charming, especially as the stalks grow longer and the flowers grow lighter.

Two things are needed for plants so treated—light and water. I used to rail when I saw all light excluded from cottage rooms by the vast collections of plants pushed into the window, but now I realize that without the light they would not thrive. House cyclamen will go on flowering for months if kept in the light and watered properly. I stand my pots of cyclamen in larger bowls which have about an inch of water in them. These stand on the low window-sill, and sometimes bloom the whole year round, but always till May and June.

Not only do flowers do better with plenty of light, they look twice as beautiful. My husband taught me this years ago, and persuaded me to put mugs of flowers right against the windows. This is easy in our house, as many of the windows have window-seats and there is a convenient ledge for the flowers.

A house like mine depends on flowers to humanize it, but it is obviously impossible to have enough fresh flowers all through the winter to make bold displays. And if one had them, they would be from a hot-house, and to me rather artificial, being so obviously out of season. I prefer leaves if I can't get anything else, such as magnolia, holly or eucalyptus. But I feel I have solved the problem by my 'deads', by which I mean dried flowers. Some people hate them, I know, just as I hate artificial flowers, but in the right kind of house and with the right kind of flowers they can be very effective.

Dried flowers mean different things to different people. I shudder when I think of the bleak stalks of yellow achillea stuck in an unimaginative vase to get more desiccated and dusty as the winter progresses, or brittle everlasting flowers (helichrysum) and mauve and yellow statice arranged in tight little posies with repellently artificial grass-green foliage.

I am not very fond either of delphiniums and larkspur, probably because I need something bolder and with more substance for the rather massive arrangements my house seems to need. Nor do the colours go so well with my mouldering walls and faded curtains as some of the things I use. Blue can be very cold in an old house, and the only larkspur I like for drying is coral, and there is never enough of it.

Dried flowers for the winter mean seed-heads for many people. Some seed-heads are colourful, others have charm, but many of them are rather dull in colour and monotonous. I prefer flowers that are picked in their prime or a moment before their prime. Teasels and Cape gooseberries *(Physalis franchetii*)* are two exceptions, and these I could not omit; most of the flowers are cut at the height of their beauty or just before, but never after. I tie the long sprays together and hang them upside down in the malthouse, which is cool and airy.

What do I use? There are so many flowers that can be used that it would be impossible to mention them all, but I will describe my favourites.

I think my favourite of all is acanthus, with its great three-foot spikes of lavender-blue flowers, each hooded with green and protected by a spiny green leaf below. The flowers fade to a deep rosy cream and the leaves to a dull green. Only a few of these impressive spikes are needed as a backbone to a really generous 'piece'. Acanthus is one of those plants with deep subterranean root works. It is not very easy to establish, and far from easy to eradicate when it gets too possessive. After being moved or divided, it will sulk for a year and produce none of its handsome massive flowers. When that happens, I have to make do with year-old-spikes when I come to do my 'deads' in the autumn.

My next choice is *Stachys lanata**, that grey woolly treasure that fulfils so many needs in our gardens. Again the spikes are three feet long and the flowers a pinky mauve. They look in death very much the same as when alive. Many of the stems are branching and have small leaves growing up them, so that not many are needed to add that lightness in colour and softness of texture which the arrangement needs.

The artemisias are a great stand-by. *A. absinthium* is the boldest, and gives great bushy sprays two and a half feet long, with myriads of tiny round flowers in light buff against fine silver leaves. *A. pontica* is a different shade of grey, rather more the colour of pewter, and the flowers are smaller and darker. I enjoy *A. pontica* in the garden, although it does increase rather rapidly. But if you are ruthless and dig up what you don't want, the result will be neat little shapely plants like miniature cypresses in ferny grey. The lightest artemisias of the lot, and I still think the best, are *A. ludoviciana* and *A. gnaphalodes**. They are practically white, and the tiny, tiny flowers are the same colour as the leaves. *A. stelleriana*'s foliage reminds one of a very silvered form of chrysanthemum, but the flowers are true to type, although golden in this case and carried in rather loose sprays. There are many more, *A. discolor**, with its threadlike foliage, and the green-leaved *A. lactiflora,* with its milk-white plumes.

The flat gold heads of *Achillea filipendula,* sometimes called 'Gold Plate', look lovely with the silvers and buffs of a big arrangement; it is only when used alone that they seem to lose their attraction. But with other things they gain in beauty, and are a great comfort to the flower arranger, as the stalks are so strong and stiff and the flowers keep their colour—for several years if necessary. There is another good yellow achillea, the Greek plant *A. clypeolata,* which is slightly more lemon in tone and far less robust than its bouncing sister. I grow it mainly for its beautiful fernlike silver foliage, but it is quite useful as a dried flower in a smaller, more dainty setting. *A. taygetea** is the colour of Devonshire cream when it first opens, but it fades to off-white. It is rather nondescript when dried, but quite useful for a background to more distinct colours. The white-flowered *A. ptarmica* drys quite well. Its little button flowers, which the villagers call 'wreath daisies', become a delicate grey and tone well with the general scheme.

*Solidaster luteus** and the new golden-rods, such as 'Lemore'* and 'Lesden', remain pale gold and keep their soft fluffiness, and they help to round off the more spiky flowers. *Limonium latifolium**, too, has a frothy effect, and although it loses some of its soft blue colour, it has a soft and soothing effect on the arrangement. Gypsophila is even more hazy, and is justly called 'baby's breath' by our American cousins. I enjoy it so much as it foams over the stones in front of the border that I am very mean when it comes to picking it. Usually I steel myself only once in the year to snip off some of that beauty, and that one haul has to last me all through the season; first in one arrangement of fresh flowers to another until the season of fresh flowers is over, and then with gratitude in the winter flower schemes. It never seems to die, and I have used the same supply two years running, when I omitted to cut it one summer.

I love the grey-leaved *Anaphalis triplinervis* for its silver foliage all the year round, and for its ivory flowers that dry so beautifully. It is a real 'immortelle', and its golden-eyed daisy flowers are a great stand-by for a large flat wooden bowl that stands on top of the tall- boy in the hall. Sometimes, the stems are not quite long enough and they are not always quite straight, but both defects are easily rectified with some fine wire.

The large form of *Physalis franchetii** is the one I grow, as it produces extra tall stalks liberally hung with outsize lanterns. Some I pick before they are quite ripe, so that the colours range from pale green through soft buff to deep orange, and I sometimes leave on a few leaves, which turn a delicate brown. Other sprays will be of intense colour, which blends so beautifully with the fawns and golds and greys of my arrangements.

One gets the same intense colour in the seed-pots of *Iris foetidissima*, our wild friend the stinking iris. They, alas, do not last as long as the other things, even when painted with gum, and in March will have to be gently drawn from the arrangements, because by then the vivid orange seeds will have shrivelled and start to fall. The flowers of this iris are not very attractive, but I know woods where they grow, so I rely on the countryside for my seed-pods, but I do grow the more attractive yellow-flowered form.

I could not manage without honesty, and I never seem to have enough when I come to arrange my 'dead' flowers. No bowl is quite right without a few pieces, but I particularly need it against the panelling in the dining-room. Here I confine my colourings to white, silver and yellow, and honesty figures very largely in the scheme. Honesty, too, is very effective with green foliage, and doesn't mind if its toes are in water sometimes instead of being dry. Very pleasant decorations can be achieved with a few sprays of honesty tucked in among the great glossy leaves of magnolia, and I find the beauty of *Garrya elliptica* is enhanced if a little honesty is introduced into the picture.

I saw two very good displays of 'dead' flowers recently which relied to a large extent on the beauty of honesty. One had a large mahogany wine cooler as the holder, and there were only three ingredients—beech leaves, yellow achillea and honesty, lots of it. The other was a more formal arrangement in a large pedestalled tureen, and again beech leaves and honesty were used, but here great masses of dried hydrangeas made the core of the decoration.

Hydrangeas are a great stand-by, and I prefer those that flower at the end of the season and often have a greenish tinge. This hint of green deepens as they dry, and sometimes they turn purple or deep madder. There is no need to hang them up to dry, as they have a pleasant habit of dying on their feet. I start them off in water, and leave them until the petals become papery and rustle when touched. Then the water is gently tipped away and the flowers are left. I usually keep them by themselves, but they can be combined very pleasantly with other flowers.

Beech leaves make a good background for any large decoration, and are quite attractive used by themselves. The secret is to cut them while they are still green and before they start to curl. Stand them in equal parts of glycerine and water until they have drunk their fill, and then use them dry. They will turn almost the colour of copper beech and are most effective. It used to be the custom to put them under a rug or carpet to make them quite flat, but it isn't necessary and gives them, I think, rather an artificial look, so I don't advocate it. Osmunda fern leaves, on the other hand, should be dried in this way if the fronds are not to curl.

There are several things I use without drying. The golden-foliaged *Cassinia* can be cut in flower and arranged in a jug, without water. The foliage doesn't change, but the small cream flowers become balls of ivory down. The downy heads of *Senecio tanguticus** look very beautiful. Some people prefer to leave them a little longer until the 'clocks' fly away, and rely on the almost irridescent skeleton of the plant. The foliage of *Senecio cineraria* lasts a very long time without withering, and outlasts many relays of fresh flowers. Other things that can be used in the same way are *Eucalyptus gunnii,* the leaves of hart's tongue fern, pieces of rue and onion heads.

The crimson plush heads of sumach are warm and sumptuous, and if I had room to grow pampas grass, I should revel in its lovely creamy plumes in my winter schemes. *Humea elegans** is a nice warm colour, and its incense fragrance is delightful in a warm room. Bulrushes I should use, too, if they grew near by,

111

and I sometimes find that the brown seed-heads of spiraea give just that depth of colour I need. Globe artichokes are handsome if they are not too top heavy for the scheme. Poppy-heads, too, are a very pleasant shade and colour. Some people paint them, and that is a sin. Crude artificial colours do not harmonize with the soft tones of our 'deads', and just kill the whole effect. I remember once seeing a most beautiful arrangement of dried flowers completely ruined by the inclusion of poppy-heads painted bright crimson, yellow and bright green. The dried flowers turn lovely soft shades, but they become dingy at once if an alien note is introduced into their midst.

Plant-Name Changes

In her writings Margery Fish naturally used the plant names that were familiar to her and which were considered acceptable at the time. But times have changed, and while many of the names she used are still current, and many that are not are nevertheless recognisable, some have changed completely.

So to help contemporary gardeners understand exactly which plants Mrs Fish is discussing, we have given the current accepted name alongside the name Mrs Fish used where we feel this is helpful. This has caused problems.

In some cases Mrs Fish gives two different names for the same plant, yet modern thinking may apply these two names to two different entities. She may also give two different names for what she asserts are two different plants yet modern thinking assures us that the two plants are the same. In some cases she indicates that one name has been superseded by another while it may now be clear that the first name, or another name altogether, is actually correct. Occasionally, Mrs Fish uses a name that has never been valid; sometimes it's clear that this is simply a misspelling, sometimes the origin of the mistake is less obvious; a little detective work has usually revealed her intent.

So while acknowledging that an entirely accurate explanation of these nomenclatural niceties would be impossible without many cumbersome footnotes, we hope that our additions will prove helpful. In identifying the correct names we sought advice and clarification from *The PlantFinder*, a range of modern encyclopedias and monographs together with expert individuals. But Mrs Fish grew such an extraordinary range of plants, some obscure even by today's standards and some now completely lost, that a few minor problems remain unresolved.

In general we have changed Mrs Fish's original text as little as possible but the accepted manner in which names are styled in type has also changed over the years. So in some cases we have simply modified the expression of an otherwise correct name in order to avoid unnecessary additions.

The science of plant nomenclature perhaps should be, but is certainly not, a precise one; however, we feel sure that by making these additions we add to an appreciation of Mrs Fish's writing and of the plants she grew.

Graham Rice

Plant name in the text	Correct current name
Achillea clavenae	Achillea clavennae
Achillea taygetea	Achillea 'Taygetea'
Ajuga reptans multicolorus	Ajuga reptans 'Multicolor'
Ajuga reptans rubra	Ajuga reptans 'Atropurpurea'
Allium mollis	Allium moly
Anaphalis nubigena	Anaphalis nepalensis var. moncephala
Anaphalis yedoensis	Anaphalis margaritacea var. yedoensis
Anthemis cupaniana	Anthemis punctata subsp. cupaniana
Antholyza	Crocosmia
Artemisia 'Lambrook Silver'	Artemisia absinthium 'Lambrook Silver'
Artemisia canescens	Artemisia alba 'Canescens'
Artemisia discolor	Artemisia michauxiana
Artemisia gnaphalodes	Artemisia ludoviciana
Artemisia lanata	Artemisia caucasica
Artemisia pedemontana	Artemisia caucasica
Artemisia 'Silver Queen'	Artemisia ludoviciana 'Silver Queen'
Artemisia splendens	Artemisia alba 'Canescens'
Artemisia tridentata	Seriphidium tridentatum
Artemisia valesiaca	Seriphidium vallesiacum
Aster yunnanensis 'Napsbury'	Aster tongolensis 'Napsbury'
Berberis thunbergii atropurpurea nana	Berberis thunbergii 'Atropurpurea Nana'
Bergenia megasea	Bergenia cordifolia
Campanula burgaltii	Campanula 'Burghaltii'
Campanula cordifolia	Campanula alliariifolia
Campanula macrantha	Campanula latifolia var. macrantha
Campanula van houttei	Campanula 'Van Houttei'
Cassinia fulvida	Cassinia leptophylla subsp. fulvida
Catananche caerulea major	Catananche caerulea 'Major'
Ceanothus veitchianus	Ceanothus x veitchianus
Centaurea gymnocarpa	Centaurea cineraria
Chamaecyparis lawsoniana fletcheri	Chamaecyparis law soniana 'Fletcheri'
Cheiranthus 'Harpur Crewe'	Erysimum 'Harper Crewe'
Cheiranthus 'Moonlight'	Erysimum 'Moonlight'
Chelone barbata	Penstemon barbatus
Chimonanthus fragrans	Chimonanthus praecox
Chionodoxa luciliae alba	Chionodoxa luciliae 'Alba'
Chionodoxa 'Pink Giant'	Chionodoxa forbesii 'Pink Giant'
Chrysanthemum haradjanii	Tanacetum haradjanii
Chrysanthemum macrophyllum	Tanacetum macrophyllum
Chrysanthemum praeteritum	Tanacetum praeteritum
Chrysanthemum ptarmicaeflorum	Tanacetum ptarmiciflorum
Clematis calycina	Clematis cirrhosa
Convolvulus mauritanicus	Convolvulus sabatius

Coronilla glauca	Coronilla valentina subsp. glauca
Corydalis cashmiriana	Corydalis cashmeriana
Cotoneaster lactea	Cotoneaster lacteus
Crocus tomasinianus	Crocus tommasinianus
Cyclamen atkinsii	Cyclamen coum 'Atkinsii'
Cyclamen europaeum	Cyclamen purpurascens
Cyclamen hederaefolium	Cyclamen hederifolium
Cyclamen hiemale	Cyclamen coum
Cyclamen ibericum	Cyclamen coum subsp. caucasicum
Cyclamen neapolitanum	Cyclamen hederifolium
Cyclamen orbiculatum	Cyclamen coum
Cyclamen verna	Cyclamen coum subsp. caucasicum
Cytisus kewensis	Cytisus x kewensis
Daphne collina	Daphne sericea Collina Group
Daphne 'Somerset'	Daphne x burkwoodii 'Somerset'
Dracocephalum sibiricum	Nepeta sibirica
Elaeagnus argentea	Elaeagnus commutata
Elaeagnus pungens aurea variegata	Elaeagnus pungens 'Variegata'
Epigaea asiaticus	Epigaea asiatica
Erica 'W. T. Rackliff'	Erica erigena 'W. T. Radcliff'
Erigeron 'Elstead Rose'	Erigeron 'Elstead Pink'
Erigeron 'Mrs Beale'	Erigeron 'Mr F. H. Beale'
Euonymus radicans	Euonymus fortunei var. radicans
Euonymus 'Silver Queen'	Euonymus fortunei 'Silver Queen'
Euphorbia Robbiae	Euphorbia amygdaloides var. robbiae
Euphorbia sibthorpii	Euphorbia characias subsp. wulfenii var. sibthorpii
Euphorbia wulfenii	Euphorbia characias subsp. wulfenii
Filipendula hexapetala	Filipendula vulgaris
Gentiana hascombensis	Gentiana septemfida var. lagodechiana 'Hascombensis'
Gentiana 'Kidbrook'	Gentiana x macaulayi 'Kidbrooke Seedling'
Gentiana macaulayi	Gentiana x macaulayi
Geranium anemonifolium	Geranium palmatum
Geranium armenum	Geranium psilostemon
Geranium atlanticum	Geranium malviflorum
Geranium cinereum subcaulescens	Geranium cinereum subsp. subcaulescens
Geranium endressii 'A. T. Johnson'	Geranium x oxonianum 'A. T. Johnson'
Geranium 'Rose Clair'	Geranium x oxonianum 'Rose Clair'
Geranium 'Wargrave'	Geranium x oxonianum 'Wargrave Pink'
Geranium grandiflorum alpinum	Geranium himalayense 'Gravetye'
Geranium 'Gravetye'	Geranium himalayense 'Gravetye'
Geranium 'Ingwersen'	Geranium macrorrhizum 'Ingwersen's

	Variety'
Geranium napuligerum	Geranium farreri
Geranium sanguinaria	Geranium sanguineum
Geranium sanguineum grandiflorum	Geranium himalayense
Geranium lancastriense	Geranium sanguineum var. striatum
Geranium stapfianum roseum	Geranium orientalitibeticum
Geranium striatum	Geranium pratense 'Striatum'
Geranium traversii 'Russell Prichard'	Geranium x riversleaianum 'Russell Prichard'
Gladiolus byzantinus	Gladiolus communis subsp. byzantinus
Gladiolus tristis grandis	Gladiolus tristis
Helenium pumilo magnifico	Helenium pumilum 'Magnificum'
Helichrysum alveolatum	Helichrysum splendidum
Helichrysum angustifoliurn	Helichrysum italicum
Helichrysum marginatum	Helichrysum milfordiae
Helichrysum trilineatum	Helichrysum splendidum
Helleborus abchasicus	Helleborus orientalis subsp. abchasicus
Helleborus atrorubens	Helleborus orientalis subsp. abchasicus 'Early Purple'
Helleborus corsicus	Helleborus argutifolius
Helleborus guttatus	Helleborus orientalis subsp. guttatus
Helleborus macranthus	Helleborus niger subsp. macranthus
Helleborus niger altifolius	Helleborus niger subsp. macranthus f. altifolius
Hieracium pilosella	Pilosella officinarum
Hieracium waldsteinii	Hieracium lanatum
Humea elegans	Calomeria amaranthoides
Hyacinthus azureus	Muscari azureum
Hyacinthus praecox album	Muscari azureum 'Album'
Hydrangea macrophylla mariesii	Hydrangea macrophylla 'Mariesii'
Hydrangea villosa	Hydrangea aspera Villosa Group
Iris alata	Iris planifolia
Iris angustifolia	Iris unguicularis subsp. carica var. angustifolia
Iris chamaeris	Iris lutescens
Iris foetidus	Iris foetidissima
Iris 'Ambassador'	Iris 'Ambassadeur'
Iris intermedia	Iris Intermediate Bearded
Iris kaempferi	Iris ensata
Iris ochroleuca	Iris orientalis
Iris 'The Bride'	Iris 'Bride'
Iris speciosus	Iris unguicularis 'Speciosa'
Iris stylosa	Iris unguicularis
Iris unguicularis angustifolia	Iris unguicularis subsp. carica var. angustifolia
Iris unguicularis speciosa	Iris unguicularis 'Speciosa'
Lamium ovata	Lamium orvala

Lamium galeobdolon luteum variegatum	Lamium galeobdolon subsp. montanum 'Florentinum'
Lapeyrousia cruenta	Anomatheca laxa
Limonium latifolium	Limonium platyphyllum
Lithospermum rosmarinifolium	Lithodora rosmarinifolia
Lychnis coronaria atrosanguinea Group	Lychnis coronaria Atrosanguinea
Lychnis coronaria 'Abbotswood Rose'	Lychnis x walkeri 'Abbotswood Rose'
Magnolia grandiflora Exbury form	Magnolia grandiflora 'Exmouth'
Mahonia bealei	Mahonia japonica Bealei Group
Mahonia lomariifolium	Mahonia lomariifolia
Marrubium candidissima	Marrubium incanum
Meconopsis baileyi	Meconopsis betonicifolia
Mentha rotundifolia variegata	Mentha suaveolens 'Variegata'
Montbretia rosea	Tritonia disticha subsp. rubrolucens
Montbretia 'Solfaterre'	Crocosmia x crocosmiflora 'Solfatare'
Muscari comosum monstrosum	Muscari comosum 'Plumosum'
Nepeta mussinii	Nepeta x faassenii
Nepeta 'Souvenir d'Andre Chaudron'	Nepeta sibirica 'Souvenir d'André Chaudron'
Othonnopsis cheirifolia	Othonna cheirifolia
Oxalis floribunda	Oxalis articulata
Penstemon campanulatus 'Evelyn'	Penstemon 'Evelyn'
Penstemon 'Garnet'	Penstemon 'Andenken an Friedrich Hahn'
Penstemon heterophyllus 'True Blue'	Penstemon heterophyllus
Phlomis 'E. C. Bowles'	Phlomis chrysophylla 'Edward Bowles'
Phlomis viscosa	Phlomis russelliana
Physalis franchetii	Physalis alkekengii var. franchetii
Polygonum affine	Persicaria affinis
Polygonum bistorta	Persicaria bistorta
Polygonum vaccinifolium	Persicaria vaccinifolia
Potentilla farreri	Potentilla fruticosa 'Gold Drop'
Potentilla 'Miss Willmott'	Potentilla nepalensis 'Miss Willmott'
Potentilla 'Mount Etna'	Potentilla 'Etna'
Potentilla 'Roxana'	Potentilla nepalensis 'Roxana'
Potentilla vilmoriniana	Potentilla fruticosa 'Vilmoriniana'
Primula alba plena	Primula vulgaris 'Alba Plena'
Primula altaica grandiflora	Primula elatior subsp. meyeri
Primula 'Bon-Accord Blue'	Primula 'Bon Accord Blue'
Primula 'Bon-Accord Gem'	Primula 'Bon Accord Gem'
Primula 'Bon-Accord Purity'	Primula 'Bon Accord Purity'
Primula 'Groeneken's Glory'	Primula 'Groenekan's Glorie'
Primula 'Madame de Pompadour'	Primula 'Madame Pompadour'
Primula 'Mrs McGilvray'	Primula 'Mrs McGillivray'

Primula 'Quaker's Bonnet'	Primula 'Lilacina Plena'
Prunella webbiana	Primula grandiflora
Prunus autumnalis	Prunus x subhirtella 'Autumnalis'
Prunus subhirtella autumnalis	Prunus x subhirtella 'Autumnalis'
Pyrus salicifolia argentea	Pyrus salicifolia 'Pendula'
Rhus cotinus Notcutt's variety	Cotinus coggygria 'Notcutt's Variety'
Rosa chinensis	Rosa x odorata 'Pallida'
Rosa chinensis mutabilis	Rosa x odorata 'Mutabilis'
Santolina neapolitana	Santolina pinnata subsp. neapolitana
Saxifraga megasea	Bergenia cordifolia
Scabious 'Clive Greaves'	Scabiosa caucasica 'Clive Greaves'
Scabious 'Miss Willmott'	Scabiosa caucasica 'Miss Willmott'
Schizostylis giganteum	Schizostylis coccinea 'Major'
Scilla tubergeniana	Scilla mischtschenkoana
Scrophularia nodosa variegata	Scrophularia auriculata 'Variegata'
Senecio compactus	Brachyglottis compacta
Senecio greyii	Brachyglottis 'Sunshine'
Senecio laxifolius	Brachyglottis 'Sunshine'
Senecio leuchostachys	Senecio viravira
Senecio monroi	Brachyglottis monroi
Senecio tanguticus	Sinacalia tangutica
Senecio 'White Diamond'	Senecio cineraria 'White Diamond'
Solidago 'Lemore'	x Solidaster luteus 'Lemore'
Solidaster luteus	x Solidaster luteus
Spiraea filipendula	Filipendula vulgaris
Spiraea flore pleno	Filipendula vulgaris 'Multiplex'
Stachys grandiflora	Stachys macrantha
Stachys lanata	Stachys byzantina
Symphytum Caucasian form	Symphytum caucasicum
Symphytum grandiflorum	Symphytum ibericum
Verbascum broussa	Verbascum bombyciferum
Verbascum haenseleri	Verbascum rotundifolium
	subsp. haenseleri
Veronica catarractae	Parahebe catarractae
Veronica cupressoides	Hebe cupressoides
Veronica edinensis	Hebe 'Edinensis'
Veronica hulkeana	Hebe hulkeana
Veronica loganioides	Hebe 'Loganioides'
Veronica 'Morning Glory'	Hebe 'Primley Gem'
Veronica salicifolia	Hebe salicifolia
Veronica teucrium trehane	Veronica prostrata 'Trehane'
Viburnum fragrans	Viburnum farreri
Vinca elegantissima	Vinca major 'Variegata'
Vinca minor alba variegata	Vinca minor 'Alba Variegata'
Vinca minor caeruleo-plena	Vinca minor 'Azurea Flore Pleno'
Vinca minor 'Celestial'	Vinca minor 'Azurea Flore Pleno'
Vinca minor 'La Graveana'	Vinca minor 'La Grave'

Vinca minor roseoplena	*Vinca minor* 'Rosea Plena'
Vinca minor rubra	*Vinca minor* 'Atropurpurea'
Viola 'Admiral Avellan'	*Viola* 'Ameril Avellan'
Viola labradorica	*Viola riviniana* Purpurea Group
Viola 'Marie Louise'	*Viola* 'Marie-Louise'
Viola odorata alba	*Viola odorata* 'Alba'
Viola pensylvanica	*Viola pubescens* var. *eriocarpa*
Viola 'Princess of Wales'	*Viola* 'Princesse de Galles'
Viola sulphurea	*Viola* 'Sulphurea'

Index

An * indicates an entry in the
Plant-name Changes section.

A

acanthus 109
Achillea
   *A. clavenae** 95
   A. clypeolata 94, 109
   A. filipendula 109
   A. ptarmica 110
   *A. taygetea** 109-10
acidantheras 35-6, 104
aconites 11-12, 30
Ageratum 81
Agrostemma 68, 94
Ajuga
   A. pyramidalis (syn. *genivensis*) 77
   A. reptans
      *A.r. multicolorus** 77
      *A.r. rubra** 77
Allium
   A. caeruleum 32
   A. giganteum 32
   *A. mollis** 32
alpine strawberries 80
Anaphalis
   A. margaritacea 94
   *A. nubigena** 94
   A. triplinervis 94, 110
   *A. yedoensis** 94
angelica 104
*Anthemis cupaniana** 18
arabis 89
Arenaria balearica 54
Artemisia 93-4
   A. absinthium 93, 109
   *A. canescens** 16, 94
   *A. discolor** 94, 109
   A. glacialis 95
   *A. gnaphalodes** 93, 109
   A. lactiflora 109
   *A. 'Lambrook Silver'** 93
   *A. lanata** (syn. *pedemontana**) 95-6
   A. ludoviciana 93, 109
   A. pontica 93, 109
   *A. 'Silver Queen'** 93
   *A. splendens** 94

A. stelleriana 93-4, 109
A. tridentata 97
*A. valesiaca** 94
Asarum canadense 80
asphodelus 85-6
Aster yunnanensis 'Napsbury'* 79
astrantia 104
atriplex 12
aubretia 89
auriculas 44
azaleas 99-100

B

Ballota pseudodictamnus 13, 90
Barrington Court 47
bedding plants 81
beech leaves 111
belladonna lilies 34, 35
Bellis
   B. perennis 66, 81
   B. 'Rob Roy' 81
*Berberis thunbergii atropurpurea nana** 90
Bergenia 13, 18, 82, 86-8
   B. ciliata 88
   B. cordifolia 87, 88
   *B. megasea** 107
   B. purpurascens 88
Bermudian snowdrop 31-2
betonica *see Stachys*
Brympton d'Evercy 92
Buddleja 'Royal Red' 70
bugle 76-7, 88, 90
   see also Ajuga
bulbs 9, 29-36
   autumn-flowering bulbs 33-5
   naturalising 30
   summer-flowering bulbs 31, 32
bulrushes 111-12

C

Calceolaria
   C. darwinii 100
   C. integrifolia 68
   C. tenella 100
camassias 31
camellias 99
Campanula